Bless you to Be

Peak Performance Leadership

Dr. Randy Shepard

Dedication

This book is dedicated to several important people:

To those who have an unquenchable thirst to make a profound and positive difference in this world—may God use this book to inspire a journey that allows you to do just that!

To my parents, Ronald and Beverly Shepard, who've provided some of the best examples of leadership I've ever known—thank you. I'll be forever grateful!

To the many great leaders I've mentioned in this book that through their books, articles, and courses have provided immeasurable guidance and inspiration during my journey as a leader. You've not only inspired and trained countless numbers of people around the world, including myself, but you have reached the place of "hero" in my view. Because you've had such a profound influence in my life, I believe it's only natural that I share with others the resources that have helped me.

Introduction

Leadership is a thrilling opportunity! However, it has significant challenges. As a leader of a team, you must keep the team motivated, challenged, focused, and efficient. In general, your team wants to have fun, be rewarded, be heard, and become better than they are. They have disagreements with each other, with their work, with the company, and with their leader. It's your task to pull it all together so they're happy and working with high energy and producing the intended outcome.

Does that sound like an impossible task? Not at all. All you need is the knowledge of how to make that happen. While you've probably heard, "Knowledge is power," it's the application of knowledge that makes things happen. Armed with the right knowledge and a teachable spirit, you'll understand how to possess the confidence that's required to successfully work with a team of people—any team or organization.

After 20 years of leadership experience, I have captured that experience in this book. I have also had the privilege of sharing it with thousands of managers and leaders of Fortune 500 companies across the country. They have used this information to compete in the field of battle and were victorious. Now, you can too!

If you'll take the time to study the material found in this book and apply it personally to your own leadership style, you'll quickly be on your way to developing the kind of team that everyone wants to join—a peak performance team.

Table of Contents

Chapter 1
Peak Performance Leadership

During the 1990's, the Chicago Bulls basketball team was in its heyday. Game after game, the team engaged in artful and skillful displays of basketball theatrics. Spinning jumps, phenomenal dunks, and precise long shots dazzled audiences nationwide. Even people who didn't like basketball enjoyed watching them play. They were so popular many of the Bulls players joined celebrities on nightly talk shows, sports shows, and even political balls. Everyone loved them, and one player's name became a household word—Michael Jordan.

From the very first day as a team member of the Chicago Bulls, Michael Jordan's talent as one of the great players of the game was readily evident. His amazing leaps, free throw line slam-dunks, and aggressive ball handling became spectacular artistry, something college and high school players couldn't wait to emulate. Though the crowds would scream out for Michael Jordan to perform more and more of his spectacular feats of basketball prowess, most people failed to realize what was really going on behind the scenes.

For Michael Jordan to do his stuff, he had to rely on a great pick by Scottie Pippen, a fabulous low-post screen by Bill Cartwright, or even a clear-out by Horace Grant. Not to take anything away from Michael's talent, but if he had not relied on these men do their jobs, he couldn't have done his.

Though Michael Jordan became legendary and the Chicago Bulls won the NBA Championships for three consecutive years, we need to remember it took them seven arduous years of planning and many thousands of hours of practice to get there. This phenomenal team and its star player didn't just start out at the pinnacle of greatness. They had to work to get there.

Like any team, they had to learn to put their trust in their coach and believe in his practice methods, no matter how unusual they seemed. They had to find their purpose as a group, become a team, discover each other's strengths and weaknesses, and in unison learn how to work together synergistically. Once they did that, they entered the peak performance zone. No one could stop them, and for three consecutive years, they were champions.

Wouldn't it be great if you could champion a peak performance team like that where you work? You simply let them out onto the floor of the office and off they go—slam dunking project after project, spinning out paperwork like there's no tomorrow, and in the end, dazzling you and every other upper level supervisor as they artfully and skillfully master their jobs.

You might be laughing as you consider your team doing these things. It might even sound ridiculous as you look around your work environment and consider your resources right now, but give the advice in this book a chance. If you'll put the principles in this book into practice, I promise you'll discover a path that can ultimately lead to a peak performance team you would have never dreamed possible.

It's been my privilege during the past 20 years to train thousands of managers and leaders throughout the country in both large and small companies. Whether I am addressing the senior executive level of the Department of Agriculture, the sales managers of AT&T, or a shoe sales manager at a local department store, the principles I shared with them are written in this book. They are a combination of my own experience, coupled with the experiences and research of many of the great leaders I've studied over the past 30 years.

As a result, many of the managers and leaders I've trained have reported to me how these principles have substantially aided them in their management and leadership careers. These concepts are an amalgamation of common sense, insight, experience; the advice of great leaders, and many powerful, eternal verities we find in life, business, and the Bible.

The purpose of this book is simple! I want to help you become a peak performance leader who can effectively build up, train, and lead a peak performance team, a team that will get the job done faster and more efficiently. No doubt, as a leader, manager, or supervisor, you'll want that too!

The reality is that you can! You've already proven yourself to be a peak performance individual. Whether you're a manager, supervisor, team leader, or pastor, you've already proven your talent and skills to the powers that be. You've convinced them that you are in some way better than your peers. You've proven your competence, reliability, and ability. You're a peak performance person, and that's exactly what it takes to get started!

If you're going to build a peak performance team in the 21st century, you've got to know what a peak performance team looks like and how it should operate. Grasping these concepts, coupled with a clearly defined view of where you want to go, is half the battle.

YOU'VE GOT TO AIM AT SOMETHING

Several years ago, Virginia State and Carolina State battled for the NCAA Championship. This game was acclaimed as one of the most thrilling championship games in college history. In the last few seconds, the game was tied. In the last play of the game, Les Hanson of Virginia took the shot from one opposite end of the court. The crowd stood in silence as the ball descended upon the hoop at the far end. Swish! Virginia won! The crowd went crazy. Fans from everywhere leaped to their feet and ran down onto the court to congratulate their team and Les Hanson.

One of the national reporters caught up with Les on the team bench and asked him how he did it. "How did you make the longest shot in college basketball history?" he asked.

With a casual smile, Les Hanson turned to the reporter and said, "Hey, that's where I was aiming!"

That's all it takes in the beginning. To get started, you must aim at something specific.

I'll provide a list of qualities that characterize a peak performance team. This model will help you shape your vision, goals, and training as you work to develop yourself and your team into a peak performance model for the 21st century.

Using the word "PERFORM" in an acrostic, here's what I have found to be some simple identifying characteristics that indicate your team is in peak performance mode:

- **P - Purpose:** Peak performance begins to take shape when your team understands and is motivated by a clearly defined common purpose. They also understand and see how their roles play an important part in accomplishing the overall purpose of the team.

- **E - Empowerment:** This happens when each team member has become a fully trained specialist in what they do. They have learned how to take the initiative in solving problems within the team, and they're committed to accomplishing the team's mission.

- **R - Relationships:** A team is only as good as the strength of its relationships between team members. In a peak performance team relationship, honest communication, good listening skills, constructive conflict resolution, and the ability to give helpful feedback are givens and are critical components to the overall health of the team. A healthy team produces healthy results.

- **F - Flexibility:** Change is inevitable in every work environment. A peak performance team must learn how to change tasks and roles as needed. They realize the importance in sharing roles for the purpose of accomplishing the team mission. They need to be ready to adapt to changes in mission and team membership.

- **O - Optimal Productivity:** For teams to perform at an optimal level, they must be participatory and creative. They are also committed to quality at the highest level, make decisions that produce the greatest results, not on personal feelings or political considerations.

- **R - Recognition:** The leader must realize the need to celebrate team successes and milestones. Individual victories and team achievements are worthy of celebration and recognition.

- **M - Morale:** The most effective peak performance teams take pride in their work. They possess an optimistic and future-oriented enthusiasm. Leaders must take the initiative to maintain team pride and continually look for techniques to keep team members motivated.

This list defines where you ultimately want to take your team. I assure you it will take some time to accomplish. In fact, I've personally learned that it takes about three years to develop a true "team" concept. When you aim at these characteristics, in time, you'll get there.

Take a few moments to write these characteristics down. Put them in front of you in a place where you are reminded of them on a daily basis. Usually, if I want to remember anything, I have to tape it to the front of my computer monitor, or frame it on a wall in my office.

I don't know of anything more exhilarating or more challenging than leading a team of people, especially when they've developed into a peak performance team. Yes, it can be stressful and challenging at times, but when you've developed your team into a peak performance model, you'll start to have fun. There is incredible synergy at high levels of team coherence. A peak performance team can accomplish twice as much with half the people. This concept is so powerful that before you think of hiring more people, you may want to ask, "Is my current team working synergistically together?"

What is synergy? Synergy is simply a form of energy where the whole equals more than the sum of the parts. In other words, if you were to nail two 2 x 4's together, instead of the two conjoined boards being twice as strong, they are now three times as strong. Have you ever heard of four people doing the work of eight effectively? This is exactly what happens when you have a team working synergistically. All the parts work harmoniously together so that the output is far greater than you would normally expect.

Whether you're the manager of a small tool shop or the supervisor of a large department store, developing a team of people who work synergistically towards peak performance status means you'll have to be personally prepared to meet the challenges ahead of you. You'll need to be intellectually and emotionally competent to meet the myriad of demands that go along with the type of leadership peak performance requires.

Having spoken to managers in various cities across the United States on the subject of leadership and having worked under a few, I've come to realize that many managers and supervisors are ill-prepared for the challenges they face. Many of them have no idea what they're getting into when they sign up for the leadership job. While many of them proudly see it as a promotion, they're often not aware of the conflicts they'll need to resolve, the communication and people skills they'll need to effectively utilize, or the various kinds of motivational stimuli they'll need to learn to keep their team running at a good, cohesive pace.

SUCCESSFUL LEADERSHIP
DOESN'T COME WITH A TITLE

Just because you've been selected to lead a team of people, doesn't mean you're good at it. In fact, you might be lousy. You may have been good at your job, but leading people takes a new level of skills you may or may not possess.

Have you ever wondered, "How in the world did that person ever get selected to lead a team of people?" I know I have. I've witnessed horrible leaders.

The fact is, there are many managers and supervisors who just don't know how to lead well. They desperately need to develop skills in this area. In fact, you might be questioning your own ability right now. Perhaps you feel as though you've been thrust into an arena of honor but without the owner's manual. Don't be discouraged! There are many leaders who've felt the same way.

Here's how it often happens for many leaders, managers, and supervisors. The first step in leadership for many of them is when upper management gives them a title of authority. They are given the title, and then thrown out there. Their boss expects them to fix everything or get the hang of it at some point in time – but not too much time.

This is what happened to my wife. She was invited to be the manager of a large and fast-moving vision center. She was excited about the opportunity. The pay was great, the people were ok, but the worst part of it all was that they offered no training at all. You can imagine how frustrated she was on her first day. It was filled with her embarrassingly trying to figure out how the whole process worked, how to run the optical equipment, and even how to run the cash register.

What this vision center gave her was a title. That's it! To say she was frustrated was an understatement. By the third day, I could tell she was ready to quit. I know women can be "hinters" but her reaction when she got inside the car was no hint. It spoke volumes! As she sat down, the tears streaming down her face, the throwing of her badge across the inside of the car, and then the burying of her head in her hands gave me clear indication this was not a happy wife.

I was broken-hearted! My wife loves to work hard and excel at everything she does. Sadly, however, she was given the title of manager and then deserted. Even though she ended up working there several years and took that vision center to its highest profit margins in the history of the store, she never did receive one day of training. She made it, but not without months of tremendous frustration. Can you relate to that?

No doubt, one of the costliest mistakes upper management can make is to find a person, any person, to plug a leadership hole. Often, when they need a manager, they go the route of least resistance. Instead of doing their job in picking the right person, they will end up picking anyone that shows some sense of knowledge or leadership. Most often, the selection process is either based on a person's tenure or on their ability to do a great job at their specific task.

When upper management resolves to only using these two traits as their only identifiable criteria for choosing the right manager, this can result in a huge mistake! As in my wife's case, I've personally witnessed many outstanding workers be thrown into the place of leadership without being properly vetted and/or trained. I've seen how a lack of vetting and training leadership has led to costly mistakes within an organization or company. The frustration level that subsequently arises both from the leader and upper management has led to many of these leaders either quitting or getting fired.

Someone humorously explained the process like this: Your boss summons you into the glorious throne room of his or her office. As you pass through the door, your innate sense of inferiority compels you to take off your shoes as you enter into "the holy of holies." You feel a little nervous. As you kneel before his or her sacred desk, your boss reaches forth and out from behind the desk they pull out the infamous "Management Excalibur Sword." Your boss then chants an initiation rite. You're not sure what is said because it's said in another language known only to a select few - which is management of course. As the rite comes to a close, it's tapped off with the words, "You are now a manager. Go hither and yon and do it!" Just then something hits you like a bolt of lightning; your body begins to pulsate, and you are now filled with all the great knowledge and wisdom and experience you'll ever need to become a successful leader of people! You have been instantaneously transformed and provided with strategies that would make a Harvard business professor green with envy. You are now a manager - a leader of people. Slowly you stumble out of the boss's office ready to go hither and yon and do it.

Is that what happened to you? Probably not! I realize that's a little melodramatic, nevertheless I think you get my point.

I couldn't begin to guess how many managers and leaders have been slapped with the mantle of leadership without being provided the adequate and essential training to becoming a leader of people. Managing people is one thing, but leading them is another! And leading a team towards a peak performance status is still quite another.

Just because you've given the title of "manager" or "supervisor" or "team leader" doesn't mean that you're going to be an effective leader within the team. You've been given a title, but it still doesn't make you a great leader.

I've shared the following example in many of my leadership conferences. Imagine an F-16 fighter pilot took you through a brief initiation rite and then said, "You are now officially an F-16 fighter pilot!" How confident would you feel about jumping into the cockpit of an F-16 and taking off? The truth is, you wouldn't do it. No doubt, you'd probably like to, but you know how dangerous an F-16 jet can be in the hands of an untrained professional. Giving you the title of an F-16 fighter pilot isn't what makes you an F-16 fighter pilot. The title doesn't make it so.

Do you know who really gives you the title? Your team! Your boss or the company may initially give this right to you, but if your team isn't going to submit to your leadership, you're not leading a single thing.

It reminds me of the guy that boldly declares, "I'm the leader!" then turns to see if anyone's following him. The truth is you aren't leading a thing until you have your team behind you. This reminds me of what Alexandre Ledru-Rollin once said, "There go my people. I must find out where they are going so I can lead them."

FIVE STAGES OF LEADERSHIP

Fortunately, over the past 30 years, the publishing world has produced countless books and articles on leadership. When I was the pastor of a fast-growing church, I relied heavily upon the expert advice from such leaders as John Maxwell, Brian Tracy, Zig Ziglar, William Cohen, and many others. Learning from these leaders, who were what I call "field tested leaders," was a huge importance to me. As the church membership expanded, I relied on their advice, as I would face new challenges. Not only did I find new challenges at various stages of church growth, but as the leader, I also found myself needing to be equal to the challenge at every level. As your team (or in this case the church) grows, you must be up to the new challenges you'll face. Challenges are not static. They are in a constant state of flux.

For example, there were certain challenges just to get the church started. After we grew to twenty-five families, new challenges and requirements stared me in the face. The same thing happens at fifty families, at a hundred families, and so on. As your team grows, you'll find your leadership being challenged by new things, new requirements that require new leadership skill sets.

I'm convinced about one thing. Being the pastor of a fast growing church is about the most leadership-intensive enterprise I've ever been involved in. If you think it's tough to get paid employees motivated to give their best, try getting volunteers at the end of the day or week to do the same!

I like how leadership expert John Maxwell, in his book The 5 Levels of Leadership, offers a general overview of "the five levels of leadership" that peak performance leaders must pass through. These levels are exactly what I've experienced either through my own leadership opportunities or through what I have observed in the development of high performing leaders in other organizations. Based on my personal experience, here is an overview of the stages you'll experience in the process of becoming a peak performance leader.

1) The first stage is the "position" stage. When you first become a leader of people, remember that you've been given a position of authority. At this point, you simply have a title. As a manager or supervisor, you've been given the mantle of leadership by position or title only. Through the decision of your boss, the company, or perhaps even the board of directors, you've been selected to lead a group of people. This makes you their leader by default. But like I said earlier, though you might be the designated leader of the group, the question to ask yourself is "Is anyone following my lead?" In reality, you're not leading anyone unless someone's following you.

When you are a "position" manager, you are at the base or entry level on the leadership scale. It means that you've either been newly selected as the team's new leader within the past couple of years, or you're having some trouble passing on to the next level. During this stage, people follow you because they have to. The longer you stay at this level, the higher the employee turnovers will become. Consequently, the morale within the group will drop significantly.

I spoke at a leadership conference in the Northeast, and during the event, a young man in his late twenties approached me immediately after the first break. For nearly ten minutes, he shared his frustrations and agony with me concerning his appointment as the new manager of a department within a large tool-and-die shop. Though he'd been with the company for several years and knew each of the men within the department, he was the new guy on the block and felt it. Even after a few months, he still didn't feel as though he had control as a manager.

Whenever he'd try to exercise his leadership within the department, they had a hard time taking him seriously as their leader. Though this young manager personally got along with everyone within the department, it was going to take some time to develop the relationship and respect that was necessary to earn true leadership within the group. He was a leader by position only. No one was seriously interested in following his lead until he proved himself and developed the relationship that was necessary to move him into the second stage of leadership.

2) The second stage is called the "permission" stage. This is called the permission stage because you are now leading by the permission granted by your team. Once your company gives you the position of leader, you don't truly begin to lead your teammates until they grant you their permission to lead them. Unless you have their permission to lead, you're only dreaming if you think you're leading.

To reach the "permission" stage of leadership, you must begin the process of developing relationships with the individuals on your team. This means you need to take the time to get to know the people on your team. You must understand their strengths and weaknesses, what values they bring to the table, and what they value in their job.

You also need to show them you care about them. Taking the time to talk with them and getting to know them is one of the best ways of showing them you care. It's been often said, "No one cares how much you know, until they first know how much you care." Your team will respond to your desires and requests with greater happiness and more zeal once they know you care.

HOW TEAM LEADERSHIP HAS EVOLVED

During the first half of the twentieth century, the concept of teams was relatively new. Things were quite different in the workforce than they are today.

In the 1950's and 60's when my father worked for General Motors, managers operated under what some have referred to as the "transactional concept." This meant the boss would transact an order and it was required that the employees implicitly follow the order. In those days, the boss didn't often associate with his or her subordinates. Employees were told what to do, and they did it. At that time, building relationships with your subordinates was seen as unnecessary.

Loyalty was another thing that was viewed differently in those days. Most workers felt the need to be loyal to the organization. To prove loyalty, they stayed with the employer for most of their career life. My grandfather worked for the postal service for more than 40 years. In fact, most men of his generation did the same. They worked for the same company, regardless of the ups and downs. It might seem strange to us today, but I assure you grandpa wasn't so strange. That was the typical mindset. During that era, most moms stayed home to care for the children while dads went to work, and stayed at the same company or job for the rest of his life.

Today's work environment is totally different! It's not uncommon for both spouses to work and to change jobs and/or careers several times in life. In my grandpa's day, if you were to show up with a resume that detailed a change of a job or a company every three to five years, you would have been labeled a rebel or an uncommitted worker. Your chances of getting a good-paying job would have been slim. That type of jumping around from job to job or company to company would have made you look unstable and unfaithful to the companies who hired you in the past.

Below, you'll find a simple chart revealing just how things have evolved over the years:

CHARACTERISTIC:	THEN:	NOW:
Attachment to employer	Long Term Employment	Short Term Employment
Readiness to change jobs	Not interested	Not looking (but will listen)
Priorities on the job	The firm and its goals	Personal life and career
Devotion to employer goals	Follows orders	Needs buy in
Effort on the job	100 percent	110 percent
Motto:	Semper Fidelis (*Always Faithful*)	Carpe diem (*Seize the day*)

As you can see, things have changed dramatically since the 1960's. The "team" concept has evolved, and with that has come the understanding of how teams work. This has been researched and written about in hundreds of magazines and books. We've learned teams work best when they operate as a unit utilizing the forces of synergy.

One of the first steps to developing a synergistically structured team is by building relationships with every member on the team. A manager who wants to be effective as a leader must get acquainted with his or her employees. It doesn't mean you have to be close friends, but a leader only receives permission to lead by building relationships with the team players.

Back in the 1970s, my dad was selected to become the general foreman for the body shop for one of the General Motors plants in the Kansas City area. At that time, it had the lowest rating in quality control of all the departments within the assembly area. The general foreman that was on his way out was also burned out and was tired of dealing with such "uncommitted" workers.

When my dad went in, the first thing he planned to do was find out why the department had the lowest rating in quality control. During the planning process, he decided he would meet with each employee and find out what they were thinking, as well as what they liked about their job versus what they didn't like. As the meetings progressed, my dad began to develop a relationship with those men within the department. Friendships were started, and the men within the body shop began to feel freedom in airing out their thoughts with my dad. As a result, quality ratings began to improve. Within three years, the body shop went from the lowest rating to the highest, simply because the men in that department felt my father cared about them. Feeling cared for, they handed their permission for him to lead them into being one of the most productive units within the plant. Remember, people don't care how much you know until they know how much you care.

In the position stage, people follow your lead because they have to. In the permission stage, people follow you because they want to.

3) The next stage of development for leaders is the "production" stage. People follow you because you get things done. You're a producer. You make things happen! You get results. Everyone loves to be where the action is, and people gravitate to winners. When you and your team produce to the extent you're reaching your goals on time and with great efficiency, it creates excitement and motivation. Your company rewards you, and you reward your team. Who wouldn't like that? When you become known as a producer, people will want to follow you!

4) The next stage is "people development." In this stage, people follow you because of what you're doing for them. In this stage, you're developing people into leaders. A leader becomes great, not because of the skills or powers they possess themselves, but because they see the value in and take the time to empower others. Success without a successor is failure.

In this stage, your team has learned to respect and honor you. They may not like or agree with everything you say or do, but they know you are someone who can get things done and you have done a lot for them personally. They have an innate sense they owe you their loyalty and service. When you empower others, you provide them with new skills and develop them into people of greater value to the organization. They will come to realize this and be appreciative. They will follow you because of what you've done for them and their career.

5) The final stage would be "personhood." This happens when you've nearly become legendary in your ability to lead people. This is something that can only happen over a long period of time. During that time, people have witnessed your ability to successfully lead a team or company to success. You've proven yourself. When you reach this stage, people automatically follow

you because of who you are and what you've done for them and the company. In essence, your name becomes synonymous with the company. Take for example, Lee Iacocca.

I remember when Lee Iacocca became the CEO of Chrysler. He was a man people followed because of his legendary know-how and ability to gather a group of leaders to build a successful enterprise. When he was asked to leave the Ford Company and become the new CEO of a struggling Chrysler Corporation in 1978, the whole Chrysler organization couldn't wait to get behind him. His outstanding reputation had preceded him. By this time, he had become a legendary leader in the automobile industry. At Chrysler, people enthusiastically followed him because of who he was. They didn't have to wait for him to prove himself. He had already done that. Based on his legendary ability and status, they knew success was right around the corner and things would change for the better. And it happened! In fact, his name was synonymous with Chrysler. You couldn't think of Chrysler without thinking of the powerful leader behind the company. Millions of people bought Chrysler cars and trucks because they believed in and trusted Lee Iacocca. I was one of them!

As you consider these five consecutive stages of leadership, keep in mind they are a general progression of steps all leaders must follow in order to effectively lead a team into peak performance status. If you're going to have a peak performance team, you must become a peak performance leader. The next chart summarizes the five levels of leadership and offers you a guided path to success within your position as a leader.

THE FIVE LEVELS OF LEADERSHIP	
1	**The Position Stage –** They follow you because they have to.
2	**The Permission Stage –** They follow you because they want to.
3	**The Production Stage –** They follow you because of what you can do.
4	**The People Stage –** They follow you because of what you've done for them.
5	**The Personhood Stage –** They follow you because of who you are.

Becoming a great leader takes time, and it takes a good deal of education. I'm not necessarily encouraging you to go back to college, but I am saying we all need to be in a progression of learning as we go. Personally, I am attracted to good books and programs on leadership. I want to be a better person tomorrow than I am today. I want to grow to my fullest potential as a human being. I believe the more I have to offer someone else, the more I can sow the seeds that can benefit others. As a good leader, you need to remember life is not as much about us as it should be about others. One of the world's greatest motivators, Zig Ziglar, said, "Give enough people what they want, and they'll give you what you want." Your job is to better yourself today so others can learn from you and grow tomorrow.

THE VALUE OF AUTOMOBILE UNIVERSITY

Zig Ziglar always included a session in his seminars on the value of attending "automobile university." He continuously stresses to his audience we should turn our twenty to thirty minute commute into a learning period. Instead of trying to use the radio to stay awake, we should be waking up to some motivation that will make us better people and stronger leaders. Ziglar strongly encouraged all of his seminar attendees to use their driving time more wisely. In one of his seminars, Ziglar describes a lady who taught herself how to speak Spanish while driving to work. As a result, she landed a better paying job and one she really enjoys. Today, there's no excuse for not using automobile university. There are many good audio books and audio programs we can take advantage of while simply driving to work.

Years ago, I found a fascinating article in the *Think and Grow Rich* newsletter. It referenced how many hours the average person uses while commuting to work each day, then summarily showed how many hours we can use in our cars each week to put to valuable use.

Notice the chart below. Imagine putting those hours to work for you. It's amazing how much a little time here and there adds up!

How Many Hours Add Up While Commuting To Work: Daily Commute (round trip) = Hours per year to learn new things

10 minutes	40 hrs.
20 minutes	80 hrs.
30 minutes	120 hrs.
40 minutes	160 hrs.
60 minutes	240 hrs.
80 minutes	320 hrs.
100 minutes	400 hrs.

LEADERS ARE LEARNERS

Unfortunately, there are a lot of people who think in order to be a great leader you must be born with the skill to lead. Yes, some people are born with more skills to lead than others, but that thought is not completely true. As leadership expert, John Maxwell, once stated: "Leadership is not an exclusive club for those who were 'born with it.'"

Bennis and Nanus, in their book *Leaders*, offer the advice: "The truth is leadership opportunities are plentiful and within the reach of most people."

Though becoming a peak performance leader might seem to be elusive, or even something that is an exclusive talent for a limited few, the truth is it is something that is primarily developed over time. And, it's not something people are automatically born with. It was Maxwell who also stated, "The truly 'born leader' will always emerge; but, to stay on top, natural leadership characteristics must be developed."

One lazy Sunday afternoon, I had the privilege of watching the training of F-16 fighter pilots on television. I was amazed to see the intensity and extensiveness of their program. In the beginning, these trainees spend countless hours and numerous weeks attending lectures and pouring themselves into books. Before they ever get into the real cockpit of a jet, they have to prove themselves worthy through countless hours of successful flight simulation. The men and women who end up as true F-16 fighter pilots do so by going through the rigorous process of thorough training and preparation beforehand. Their very lives and careers are at stake.

But so is yours! To be a successful leader, you have to take leadership seriously. No leader has ever succeeded without being willing to learn how to do it and to perform more effectively. All great leaders are great learners. They study the leadership skills and traits of others, and they constantly evaluate themselves. They discover their abilities and build on them, and work on their limitations. They don't focus on their limitations, or on the limitations others place on them. They focus on what they can do, and they work to do it better than anyone else!

Speaking of limitations, I found a ridiculous article a number of years ago that stated researchers had found people have a better chance of becoming a leader in an organization if they were taller than six feet. I had to laugh! Can you imagine what would have happened to Napoleon Bonaparte, who was a very short man, if he had believed that report? Or what about Gandhi, Harry S Truman, Ulysses S. Grant, and many others who never made it past six feet in height? One of the unique features of these great leaders is they didn't let their small stature get in the way of standing tall in front of other men, nor did they allow others to place limitations on them.

Regardless of your height, weight, or lack of education or abilities, the most important thing every great leader has had to learn at some point is to discover their abilities, to build upon those abilities, and to develop them into a beautiful and harmonic symphony of action.

WHAT IS LEADERSHIP?

Before we go any further, I'd like to take a moment to define leadership. By offering a definition, this might help us gain a glimpse of what we really need to do to become as leaders. While searching for a variety of definitions, I realized the bookstore offered a wide variety of books on leadership, which, in turn, offered their own version, or definition of leadership. George Barna of the Barna Research Group in Oxnard, California wrote one book in particular that attracted my attention. In his book, *Leaders on Leadership*, he offers a half a dozen definitions from some of America's foremost and experienced leaders. Here are three definitions I think merit our consideration:

Vance Packard defines leadership as "getting others to want to do something that you are convinced should be done."

J. Oswald Sanders says, "Leadership is influence."

Garry Wills defines it as "mobilizing others toward a goal shared by the leader and followers."

In his book, *The Art of a Leader*, William A. Cohen offers his definition as "the art of influencing others to their maximum performance to accomplish any task, objective, or project."

No matter how you slice it, leadership is more than being in a position offered by your organization. It includes the ability to influence others and work with your team to accomplish a given task or purpose as set forth by your organization. President Harry S Truman said, "I learned that a great leader is a man who has the ability to get other people to do what they don't want to do and like it."

From the definitions above, Barna goes on to share several key attributes he feels effectively describes a leader.

1. **The ability to mobilize people.** Simply put, leaders mobilize. They learn what motivates people and they get them mobilized to do the task.

2. **The ability to influence. Leaders influence people.** Sociologists tell us even the most introverted individual will influence ten thousand other people during his or her lifetime! The issue then is not whether you'll influence someone, but rather what kind of an influencer will you be?

3. **Goal driven.** A leader always keeps the end in sight and makes sure his or her team is focused on the goal.

4. **Have an orientation in common with those who rely upon the leader.** A leader must condescend to the level of his teammates and communicate with them. A leader does not take upon his or herself a "higher than thou" mentality. A leader is humble before his team and seeks to serve them. As a leader serves his team and helps them to accomplish their goals, the team will serve the leader to accomplish the overall team goal.

Without question, the greatest leader of men the world has ever known is Jesus of Nazareth. His ability to mobilize and influence has never waned. Today, millions of people follow his lead. As a great leader, he took the time to condescend to men of low estate and to serve those around him. He commanded his followers to do the same. One day he stressed to His disciples, "But he that is greatest among you shall be your servant." (Matthew 23:11) KJV

The secret of any team's success and even its downfall begins with the leader. If a team is going to be peak performance team, the principal cornerstone behind its success will be that of a peak performance leader. A peak performance leader sets the stage for a peak performance team.

One of Hollywood's most inspirational films is the movie *Hoosiers*. Set in the tiny town of Hickory, Indiana, *Hoosiers* is based on the true story about a group of basketball players at Milan High School and their exciting adventure from small-town obscurity to statewide fame. This incredibly uplifting film centers on Milan's new high school basketball coach, Norman Dale (Gene Hackman), and his struggle to deal with the challenges of becoming a new coach in an old school. Having been a former college basketball coach, Dale is asked by a friend to take over as the new head basketball coach for Milan High School. Dale agrees, but quickly realizes his greatest struggle will be gaining respect from the team players and with the people of Hickory as well. With the townspeople plagued by the "we've always done it that way" syndrome, Dale's stern and methodical methods leave no place for the fans of Hickory to provide instructional input as they did with the school's former coach.

Coach Dale faces several problems. The first thing he has overcome is the team's identification and intimate relationship with their former coach who unsuspectingly passed away the year before. Secondly, he grapples with the arduous challenge of needing to prove his competence as a successful leader and coach, not only to the team but also to the people of Hickory. Remember, this is Indiana, where babies get a round ball before a rattle. The road for Coach Dale and the team is a long one, but in the end, it produces the fruits of victory, the 1954 Indiana State Championship.

How did they do it? This small group banded together, eventually believed in their coach and became a team—a peak performance team. They worked together so well they became the best in the state of Indiana!

Peak performance leaders know how to mobilize their team members. They've built a relationship with them and know how to influence them and empower them for greater results. They've set before the team a clear goal and they lead the way by example.

Now that you have a general idea of what a peak performance team and leader looks like, let's get into more detail the essential qualities every leader must possess in order to make it all happen.

Chapter 2
The Three Essentials
Every Leader Must Possess

On May 29, 1953, Sir Edmund Hillary became the first man to scale Mount Everest-the highest mountain then known to man, some 29,028 feet straight up. Knighted for his accomplishment, Hillary's name became a household word. What many people don't realize, however, is that Hillary failed before he succeeded. In 1952, he attempted to scale Everest and didn't make it. Hillary's eventual success was directly attributed to his determination.

Three weeks after his failed attempt in 1952, Hillary gave a speech in England. When he walked on stage, the audience gave him a thunderous ovation. Even though he had failed, the crowd cheered his attempt at greatness. But that's not how Hillary saw it. He moved away from the microphone, walked to the edge of the speaking platform, and pointed to a picture of Mount Everest that was hanging on the wall. Then he said, in a loud voice so everyone could hear him, "Mount Everest, you beat me the first time, but I'll beat you the next time because you've grown all you are going to grow...yet I'm still growing!"

Though Sir Edmund Hillary failed at his first attempt, he never stopped growing and learning. Though he failed, he failed forward!

COMMIT YOURSELF TO PERSONAL GROWTH

To have the right stuff to lead a team towards peak performance, every leader must gear up to have the right stuff for effective leadership. When you study peak performance leaders, like Sir Edmund Hillary, they all seem to possess the same three characteristics. These three characteristics are essential in building a peak performance team.

The first characteristic is, as Hillary put it, an innate inward craving for personal growth. No matter how you look at it, the following is a true statement - if you grow the leader, you grow the organization. I like what George Bernard Shaw said, "I dread success. To have succeeded is to have finished one's business on earth, like the male spider that is killed by the female the moment he has succeeded in his courtship. I like the state of continual becoming, with a goal in front and not behind."

Have you noticed that no one is impressed with stagnancy? As a leader, you lose respect from the team if they don't see that you are stretching the limits of your competency. Growth is essential in the life of a leader! One of the most common and costliest mistakes is to think that successful leadership is due to some genius or some magical formula we don't quite yet possess. Successful leadership, in every culture, in every organization, and at every level comes by way of growth. If you are going to be a peak performance leader leading a peak performance team, you will have to have a proactive determination to grow. You need to get curious about life and business.

It was famous filmmaker and Disneyland founder Walt Disney who said, "We keep moving forward, opening new doors and doing new things, because we're curious and curiosity keeps leading us down new paths."

Like rubber bands, leaders come in all shapes and sizes and colors, but unless they are stretched, it's difficult for them to be useful.

The reality about stretching and growing, however, is that most people would rather do anything else rather than find themselves in a constant state of flux. And, there are several common preventable factors that are at the root of its unforgivable cause.

OVERCOMING OBSTACLES TO GROWTH

There are several reasons why most people never really commit themselves to personal growth and development after high school or college. One of the first reasons that comes to mind is that many people aren't in a growth mode. They don't see the value of growing.

Famed novelist, William Burroughs, once noted, "When you stop growing you start dying." It was Lou Holtz, former college football coach of Notre Dame now turned author and motivational speaker, who said, "In this world you're either growing or you're dying so get in motion and grow."

If you aren't reading books, attending seminars, and adding to your knowledge in the field of your career as a leader, you will get left behind. Why? In order to keep that competitive edge, you must learn and grow.

FIND YOUR REASON TO GROW

Another reason why people aren't growing is simply because nobody is challenging them to grow.

Remember when we were in school? Did we really have an inner craving to jump out of bed, throw on some clothes and get to school every day so that we could learn? Not really. The truth is, we had to. Our parents made us go, and I'm glad we did!

As I look at the workforce today, I see many people who lack an inner motivation to stretch themselves beyond their comfort zone. The idea to develop themselves mentally, socially, physically, and in leadership, seems to be a foreign idea. Sadly, what many of us need is someone to challenge us, to push us forward, to propel us to a higher level of productively and fulfillment both personally and professionally.

However, personal and professional development doesn't come easy. It's something we must make a grit-iron determination to do. As we engage in it and continue to work on it, the desire to grow will eventually become an inner desire and a daily habit.

Several years ago, at the age of 32, I decided I wanted to be competent in the new task I was about ready to undertake. For the previous twelve years, I had the wonderful opportunity and career of being a motivational and inspirational speaker. Believe me, it was not a career I had planned on.

It began during my teenage years when I was involved with a large, local youth ministry in Kansas City called Kansas City Youth For Christ. At the age of 15, I reluctantly joined a preacher boy's club that was taught by its founder, Dr. Al Metsker. This giant of a man instilled within all of us boys the need to proclaim the good news about God at any time and everywhere, to aim high in our future, and to bring ourselves into a constant state of growth. Dr. Al, (as he was affectionately called) was a phenomenal mentor for thousands of us guys during our teen years. During my high school years, he allowed me the privilege of speaking to hundreds of teenagers in nearly two hundred speaking engagements throughout Missouri and Kansas. What a wonderful time it was! Due to the number of speaking opportunities I was afforded, I decided to quit my position as the running back for our high school football team. It was a tough decision, but one that I've never regretted.

Within the next five years, I joined the staff of Youth For Christ, and Dr. Al sent me all over the country speaking in a variety of churches, high schools, organizations, and on radio and television. Everything happened fast.

During those early years as a motivational speaker, I traveled extensively, and being as young as I was, I hadn't developed the skills and disciplines I needed to further my growth and study habits. It was finally at the age of thirty-two that I realized I needed to be prepared for the challenges ahead of me.

I decided to get on the path to growing both mentally, spiritually, and in my leadership capacities. I bought books; listened to every great leader I could listen to, and gleaned wisdom from everyone older than me. In time, my craving and appetite for knowledge was a part of me, and I enjoyed what I personally and professionally gained from it. Since I was studying and researching anyway, I decided I would get some college credit for it along the way. Eleven years later I was able to graduate with a Ph.D. in Biblical Studies and Christian Counseling.

If someone had told me in the beginning that I would end up with a Ph.D., I would have died laughing. However, as a result, I've been privileged to educate and train tens of thousands of managers and leaders in various Fortune 500 companies, churches, and organizations throughout the United States, Canada, and Mexico. I've also had the opportunity to start one of America's fastest growing churches, develop a couple of successful business ventures, and become a writer.

Never once did I dream that all of these things would take place in my life. It's amazing what growth will do! If an organization is going to grow, the leader must grow. Grow the leader, grow the organization.

GET OUT OF YOUR COMFORT ZONE

Another reason why I believe people don't get into the process of growing is because of comfort. Most people are comfortable where they are. To grow and stretch themselves means they must change and do things they're normally not accustomed to doing. It also means attempting great feats by faith.

Asked about her challenges with personal growth, famous singer and actress Barbra Streisand said, "I can say, 'I am terribly frightened, and it makes me uncomfortable, so I won't do that because it's uncomfortable.' Or I can say, 'Get used to being uncomfortable. It's uncomfortable doing something that's risky.' But so what? Do you want to stagnate and just be comfortable?"

I want to encourage you to get out of your comfort zone and grow. Grow, because you can. Don't be afraid to go out on a limb; that's where the fruit is!

DON'T LET MENTAL BARRIERS GET IN THE WAY

In the movie *Good Will Hunting*, an "uneducated" janitor solves complex mathematical problems that the best and brightest MIT students couldn't figure out. George Dantzig, a professor at Stanford University, has a similar story—only his is real!

When Dantzig was a mathematics graduate student at the University of California Berkley, he was usually late for many of his classes. One day, after arriving at math class late, as usual, he saw two math problems on the blackboard. Assuming that these problems were the next homework assignment, he copied them down in his notebook. When he started working on them, he soon realized that they were much harder than the normal homework given out by the teacher. He kept plugging away, though, and after a few days, he finally made a breakthrough. Eventually, he solved both problems.

Proud of his work, he dropped the assignment on his professor's desk before the next class. Six weeks later, a furious pounding at his door awakened Dantzig on a Sunday morning. It was his mathematics professor. "George!" the man screamed. "You solved them!"

"Of course I solved them," replied Dantzig. "Wasn't I supposed to?"

The professor explained that the two problems on the board that day was not homework. They were two famous mathematical problems that nobody had ever been able to solve. Some of the leading mathematicians in the world had worked on these problems, explained the professor, but to no avail. It was a miracle that Dantzig had solved them both in only a couple of days.

Dantzig performed the impossible because he was not afraid to grow and get out of his comfort zone. Actually, he didn't know that he was going to have to really stretch for this one to work. Later, he explained why he was able to do it. He said, "If someone had told me that they were two famous unsolved problems, I probably wouldn't have even tried to solve them."

Dantzig proved the power of positive thinking. If you think you can, you can. If you think can't, you're right! Don't let the mental roadblock of comfortable conformity keep you from being all you can be.

DON'T BE AFRAID TO FAIL

I believe a third reason why many leaders are reluctant to grow is because they're afraid of what will be expected of them in the future.

My daughter Lindsey was a good example of that. She did wonderfully in school. She studied hard, made good grades, developed friendships with her teachers, and made the principal's honor roll several times. However, many of us didn't realize that she was really struggling with her success as a student. Every day, she felt the insurmountable pressure of keeping up with her grades. She loved the praise her mom and I gave her as we congratulated her successes. However, something deep inside was bothering her.

One evening, when I passed by my daughter's bedroom, I heard her crying behind closed doors. Like any concerned parent, I knocked on the door and asked to visit with her. She invited me in, and we entered into a conversation about this very issue. I had no idea she felt anxiety on the inside. What caused the anxiety was her having some difficulty in a couple of very tough subjects. She was horrified that her grades would be less than an A. She agonized over it for weeks. Lovingly, I reassured her that she had nothing to be worried about, yet it reminded me of how often many people are afraid to grow due to the challenge of keeping pace with excellence.

No leader, especially those who desire to be great and effective leaders, will be perfect in their leadership. There will be mistakes, bad decisions, lost opportunity, and disappointed team players, but people who succeed in business are able to put all those things behind them and continue to grow in spite of the bumps in the road.

If you spend too much time reflecting on your liabilities as a leader or your past mistakes or even your future challenges, it will affect your ability to recognize opportunity when it comes along. For example, here's the true story of how one man's fear of making a mistake led to his missing a great opportunity:

STOP DWELLING ON PAST MISTAKES

If you've ever listened to the History Channel, you've been enriched by the some of the biographies of great people of our past. One of those biographies I happened to enjoy one day was about Mark Twain. Twain had always had bad luck with investments. In fact, over time he had lost great sums of money while investing in one goofy invention after another. One day, a tall, thin man came to Twain's house carrying a strange looking box under his arm. Twain let the man in, and they sat down to chat. The man explained what the box was, and yes, it was an invention. Twain, who had been burned so often before, barely even listened to the man discuss the future possibilities of his invention. Twain declined to invest any money into it.

Still, the inventor persisted, saying that he only needed Twain to invest a small amount of money. But gun-shy as he was, Twain refused to get involved. As the man disappointedly walked away, the great writer called out to him:" What did you say your name was?"

"Bell," replied the inventor. "Alexander Graham Bell."

We can shake our heads as we realize Twain's great loss of opportunity in partnering with the inventor of the telephone. Here was truly the one great opportunity that would have turned everything around for him. Sadly, he missed it due to his focus on his past mistakes. While many people may have responded as Twain did when he allowed the fear of repeating past mistakes make a decision for him, the truth is we learn from our mistakes. Mistakes are an integral part of life. They aren't failures, but rather pathways to becoming better, wiser, and more efficient. But

Twain let his past misfortune rule him instead of looking to future possibilities. His future possibilities were tainted by his fear of the past.

Don't be afraid to make a mistake. A leader is making is completely naive if they think that great leaders don't make mistakes from time to time.

If you do make a mistake, be willing to admit it. You're just kidding yourself and distancing yourself from reality and your teammates if you don't recognize and own up to your own mistakes.

THE MAGIC OF RESPONSIBILITY

George "Bear" Bryant used to say, "I'm just a plow hand from Arkansas, but I have learned how to hold a team together - how to lift some men up, how to calm others down, until finally, they've got one heartbeat together as a team. There's always just three things I say: *'If anything goes bad, I did it. If anything goes semi-good, then we did it. If anything goes real good, they did it.'* That's all it takes to get people to win." Bryant, as great as he was, wasn't afraid to admit to his mistakes. In fact, he took ownership in the loss experienced by his team. His team, in turn, developed great admiration for the man.

Most people don't know that John F. Kennedy hit his highest level of popularity after he flubbed the Bay of Pigs. It doesn't seem to make sense, but JFK actually gained a ton of popularity after demonstrating to the world that he had feet of clay. Psychologists call this maneuver a "strategic-pratfall effect." By botching the invasion, and then being quick to accept responsibility for it, Kennedy showed the public not only that he was human, but was susceptible to making mistakes, too. He also showed that he was honest and upright about owning up to them. Therefore, when you make a mistake, admit it, but don't let it cause you to skew your outlook for future opportunities. So you've made mistakes. So what! Move forward! Don't let fear grip you like it did Twain. As Pema Chadron says, from her book *When Things Fall Apart*, "Fear is a natural reaction to moving closer to the truth."

When the Columbia shuttle disintegrated on its re-entry into the earth's atmosphere, our nation was stunned. As our nation mourned over their death and prayed diligently for the astronaut's families, many people in our country seriously doubted the future of manned space travel. CNN reported an uproar among some Americans who demanded that NASA completely dismantle the manned space program and eliminate its future. There have been more successful space flights than there have been failed ones, and despite the fact that we are enjoying more than 30,000 new products due to manned experiments in space, there are some who focus on the few failures rather than on the enormous benefits manned space travel has provided.

Even though the value of human life is priceless and the loss of human life is tragic, should we totally disregard what these wonderfully brave men and women have done in sacrificing their lives to accomplish these great feats? Though this might sound a little trite, should we dismantle and eliminate the manned automobile program simply because thousands of people die each year in them? The point is this, if we focus more on our failures more so than we do the opportunities that lay ahead of us, we'll miss out on huge benefits.

If you've experience a bad situation, evaluate the incident, then move on to make the right decision the next time. Turn the negative energy you feel into positive energy. As leadership writer, Brian Wilson, puts it, "In the long run, the most important results of leadership are not what we achieve but what we become in that achieving."

LEADERS SET THE PACE

My experience is that all effective leaders must have a peak performance standard. After all, performance is the reason you are a leader. As a part of a leadership standard, leaders know why something must be done. Remember, the person who knows how will always have a job, but the person who knows why will always be his boss. Leaders must learn not only the why of the job, but they must perform the why at their best ability. Leaders must also learn to motivate their team to perform the how at the team's highest ability level. When leaders use this standard, then leaders set the pace.

When leaders inspire other people to perform at their highest level, the leaders must set a standard of excellence by their work pace. Plus, they must articulate the team goals consistently in their discussions with the team. For example, Chrysler president Lee Iacocca, is known to have often repeated to his executive staff that, "The speed of the boss is the speed of the team." Leaders set the pace in all discussions.

EVERYTHING RISES AND FALLS ON LEADERSHIP

Since everything (production, quality control, efficiency, etc.) and everyone (team output, team unity, etc.) relates back to the leader, everything rises and falls on leadership. Bad leadership produces bad results. Great leadership produces great results. It's that simple. Therefore, with this being true, the standard of excellence must begin with you, the leader. When you maintain a high level of performance, it helps bring the team to an acute awareness of the standard that is expected from you and from the organization you represent. You represent and model your company's code of conduct. What they see in you, they will emulate. Since people generally never rise above the level of their leader, it is more likely that your team will perform at a slightly lower level

Let me illustrate. On a scale of one to ten, if a leader sets the standard of performance for himself at an eight, the performance outcome of the team will more than likely be a five or a six. If you're going to expect a higher level of performance from your team, you must set the standard high with yourself first. Once this is done, the message will transcend itself to the team. Nobody is perfect, yet you still need to strive for perfection.

I'm not saying that you demand it of them, but that you expect it from them because you expect it out of yourself. If you shoot for a ten, this will bring your team up to a level of a seven, or an eight, or perhaps even a nine.

There's nothing wrong with striving for perfection. Can you imagine if some leaders in certain particular industries decided that 99.9% was good enough? What do you think the outcome would be? Here's how one company describes it. In an article written in InSight from the Syncrude Canada Ltd Communications Division, those surprising and disturbing results were recorded:

If 99.9% is good enough, then...

- 12 babies will be given to the wrong parents each day.

- 22,000 checks will be deducted from the wrong bank account in the next 60 minutes.

- The IRS will lose 2 million documents this year.

- 291 pacemaker operations will be performed incorrectly this year.

- 2 plane landings at O'Hare International Airport in Chicago will be unsafe each day.

- 55 malfunctioning automatic teller machines will be installed this year.

- And 880,000 credit cards in circulation will turn out to have incorrect cardholder information on their magnetic strips.

For some industries, 99.9% can result in tragedy. What about yours?

Recently, an article in our local newspaper gripped me as it told the story of how a 17-year old was given the wrong heart and lungs in a major transplant operation in a hospital in Durham, North Carolina. How could something like this go wrong? Simple. Someone mistakenly typed in the wrong blood type. Just one letter off and a young girl has lost her life. Now there's a lawsuit.

Your organization may not demand this type of scrutiny, but the point is that mistakes can cost a company hundreds and even thousands of dollars. Minimizing mistakes is part of making a peak performance team.

THE POWER OF INTEGRITY

Another characteristic that all leaders have within them is the need to maintain a high standard of moral and ethical practice. Quite frankly, honesty and integrity are good business! Coach John Wooden once said, "Be more concerned with your character than your reputation, because your character is what you really are, while your reputation is merely what others think you are."

American educators, Warren G. Bennis and Burt Nanus, in delineating the difference between a manager and a leader said, "Managers are people who do things right, and leaders are people who do the right thing."

When J.C. Penney opened his first dry goods store in Kemmerer, Wyoming in 1902, he named it "The Golden Rule." Why? Because "Golden Rule principles are just as necessary for operating a business profitably as are trucks, typewriters, or twine," he said. Penney always wore a lapel button with the letter HCSC on it. The stood for "Honor, Confidence, Service, Cooperation." Those words come from Penney's "Original Body of Doctrine," which says:

- To expect for the service, we render a fair remuneration and not all the profit the traffic will bear.

- To serve the public as nearly as we can to its complete satisfaction.

- To offer the best possible dollar's worth of quality and value.

- To strive constantly for a high level of intelligent and helpful service.

- To apply this test to everything we do: Does it square with what is right and just?

By 1907, J.C. Penney had a chain of 22 stores, and for the next 100 years, his company would become a household word throughout America.

Integrity is everything in business. Without it, you can't be trusted. And, when you've breached the trust factor, relationships crumble. Beware of the "Madison Avenue Mentality" which believes that anything is right if the public can be convinced it is right; being more concerned with appearing ethical than being ethical; exploiting workers and cutting corners on quality to benefit the almighty bottom line.

LEADERS MUST BE ETHICAL

In a survey of corporate managers conducted by the American Society for Quality Control, an astonishing report was issued that exemplifies the serious ethical concerns we are experiencing in the American workforce today. Here's what they had to say:

- Most managers believe they face ethical problems.

- Most managers believe they and their employees should be more ethical.

- Some managers lower their ethical standards to meet job requirements.

- Most managers are aware of unethical practices in their companies and in their industries.

- Business ethics can be influenced by management and by the company environment.

LEADERS MUST BE HONEST

Wouldn't it be great if everyone in baseball today practiced the honesty of Ted Williams? More than 30 years ago, Ted Williams was closing out his career with the Boston Red Sox. He was suffering from a pinched nerve in his neck that season. "The thing was so bad," he later explained, "that I could hardly turn my head to look at the pitcher."

For the first time in his career, he batted under .300, hitting just .254 with 10 home runs. He was the highest-salaried player in sports, making $125,000. The next year, the Red Sox sent him the same contract.

When he got the contract, Williams sent it back with a note saying that he would not sign it until they gave him the full pay cut allowed. "I was always treated fairly by the Red Sox when it came to contracts," Williams said. "Now they were offering me a contract I didn't deserve. And I only wanted what I deserved."

Williams cut his own salary by 25 percent, raised his batting average by 62 points, and closed out a brilliant career by hitting a home run in his final time at bat.

Wouldn't it be awesome if every professional athlete approached his career like that? Better yet, wouldn't it be wonderful if every CEO, president, and employee operated with such honesty and integrity?

According to *The Power of Ethical Management*, authors Norman Vincent Peale and Ken Blanchard recommend the following advice whenever you're faced with a tough, ethical decision. You should ask these questions:

1. Is it legal? Will you be violating either company policy or civil law?

2. Is it fair and balanced? Are all the people involved in the decision being treated fairly in both the short term and the long term? Will certain individuals get hurt?

3. How will you feel when it's done? How will the decision make you feel about yourself? Will you be proud of what you did? If it were published in the newspaper, would you feel good about your friends and family reading it?

An article I read in the *Power of Positive Leadership* newsletter distributed by Regan Communications in Chicago offered the idea of writing a news story about yourself and your team to see if you're staying ethical. It suggested that at the end of every month (or week, if time permits) you write a short "news story" about you and your team's work-related decisions. Don't worry about the quality of the writing, just capture the highlights of what you did. For example, reviewing employees, disciplining employees, running meetings, dealing with supervisors, handing out praise and criticism, etc. Then, look at your story. Would you be comfortable if it ran in your local paper? If you have no problem publishing your story every month, odds are you are leading your team in an ethical manner.

Miriam Hamilton Keare outlined "The 12 Golden Rules for Living." Although they apply to life in general, they also serve as a good set of rules to follow in the workplace:

- If you open it, close it.

- If you turn it on, turn it off.

- If you unlock it, lock it up.

- If you break it, admit it.

- If you can't fix it, call in someone who can.

- If you borrow it, return it.

- If you value it, take care of it.

- If you make a mess, clean it up.

- If you move it, put it back

- If it belongs to someone else, get permission to use it.

- If you don't know how to operate it, leave it alone.

- If it's none of your business, don't ask questions.

Remember, everything rises and falls on leadership. Ethics and morality begin with the leader. However, if you should want some support, find an executive in your company whose values and principles you admire. Ask that person to address your employees in a meeting. Perhaps coordinate a lunch-and-learn. Invite the executive to cover topics such as the importance of ethics in business; how to make principle-led decisions, some of the ethical situations facing the company; real-life examples of how principles helped his or her career, or any other topic you see the need to discuss with your team.

Chapter 3
Coaching Your Team
Into Peak Performance

I'll never forget how, in 1992, our nation was headed to the Olympics with the most exciting group of basketball players to ever play the game. In fact, the headlines of every major newspaper and periodical heralded them "America's Dream Team". The entire United States watched in awe as their basketball heroes, Michael Jordan, Magic Johnson, Charles Barkley, Larry Bird, and several other basketball greats were put together to form one of the greatest teams to ever come together. When people watched them play, the question was not whether they would win or lose. The question was, "What magnificent plays will I see, and how wide will the winning margin be?" The team was a phenomenal assembly of stars that caused even the opposing players to ask for their autographs. As they played before the eyes of the world, they stunned everyone with their great, formidable power and basketball theatrics.

Can you imagine having a team like that working for you? I can only imagine that all leaders dream of having a team like that - players who know the game inside out, who have the talent, the desire, and the discipline to compete and succeed on the highest level. Unfortunately, most leaders don't believe that having a team like that will ever happen to them. And, for many of them, they're probably right. Why? Because they don't know how to coach people the right way - a way that leads down a road that ensures everyone of their success.

THE COACH APPROACH

Banker Walter Wriston, in *Harvard Business Review*, once said, "The person who figures out how to harness the collective genius of the people in his or her organization is going to blow the competition away!" That's what a leader/coach does! He or she harnesses the collective genius of the team, places them where they will perform the best, and leads them down the path toward personal success.

In the many conferences that I've had the privilege of speaking in over the years, I've asked the audience to describe the difference they see between a manager and a coach. I'll ask them, "What comes to your mind when I say the word "manager?" Invariably, the response is "Boss, head honcho, hirer and firer, overseer, supervisor, dictator, company representative." What I find most unique in their feedback is that it's almost always viewed as something negative. When they see the word "manager" or think of someone as being such, the mental image that flashes through their mind is not necessarily a positive one.

Then, I'll ask them, "What comes to your mind when I say the word "coach?" Immediately, you can see a more uplifting, visual response in their faces. There's almost a smile as they think back to a time when they were coached by one of the dads in little league sports or a teacher that took some time to nurture them, or someone who had some meaningful influence in their life. The words that fly out of their mouths are usually the same: "Leader, motivator, mentor, competent teacher, trainer, friend, inspirer, challenger." You can almost feel their conviction as they describe their impression of a coach. Invariably, the word "coach" or the thought of one generally brings to the forefront of people's minds a positive image.

If that's the case, then let me ask you, if you had to choose between these two words whereby your team would best describe your leadership style, which would you prefer?

In my opinion, a coach is a positive, motivating influence on people. They are leaders who seek with all of their heart and with great passion to sow the seeds that benefit others. They have only one desire, and that is to win. There are no other goals or options. They have one job, and that's to win at all cost. To do that, they know that their primary responsibility will be that of making other people successful. They are confident and knowledgeable about what they do and what the team must accomplish, and with a deep-seated passion and grit-iron determination they will do all they can to bring out the potential of others.

I know what a coach is. I am one. I've made it my life's goal to help others find their God-given talents, to discover what they're designed to do, and to help provide them with knowledge and the resources to make their personal and professional lives more fulfilled. I've traveled countless miles, stayed in innumerable hotel rooms, and trained nearly a quarter of a million people in three countries in an attempt to help them reach their God-given potential. I've sacrificed countless nights away from my family, all for the sake of knowing that I could make a difference in someone's life. I'm a coach, and that what a coach does!

Take a moment to do the following coaching self-assessment test. See how well you do.

COACHING SELF-ASSESSMENT TEST

	TRUE	FALSE
Our team has mutually agreed-upon goals, and the members are motivated.		
Only the tough problems are brought to my attention.		
My group is willing to put out extra effort when needed.		
I enjoy using praise, and I use it often.		
Workflow isn't interrupted when I'm out of the office.		
I provide an environment for win-win relationships.		
My team is open to change.		
I'm known as a fair manager.		
I'm known as a supportive leader.		
I speak loudly and often of my team's achievements.		
I provide an environment for open communications.		
I encourage employees to take the lead in problem solving.		
I strive to help employees reach their fullest potential.		
I don't hesitate to be active in employee training.		
My team understands and can articulate our vision and mission.		

So, from the test, would you say that you're a coach?

To be the leader of a peak performance team you must become a great coach. When you do, you become one step closer to building the seeds to your success! *Remember, you can't be successful unless your team is successful.* Your team reflects your leadership. If your team flops, who is your supervisor going to come to? You!

This may be a bit hard to swallow, but you need your team more than they need you. You might stumble a little bit on this statement but think about it. If you were out with the flu for two weeks, how much work would get done? 90%? 80%? 70%? Would the team's workflow be somewhat effected? Yes, maybe to some extent. However, let's turn the tables and ask the question, "If your whole team was out with the flu for two weeks, how much would get done? 20%? 30%?

Do you see what I mean? Without your team, it becomes extremely difficult to reach your workload objectives. In summary, without the aid of your team, productivity takes a huge dive.

Here's another way to look at it. How many games would a basketball coach win without its players? None! *Your team determines your success.* That's why you want to do all that you can to develop a peak performance team!

While traveling around the country addressing the many managers and supervisors I've had the privilege of training, I've asked them what they thought were some of the signs of a great coach. The following is a list of those things that have come from hundreds of top-level leaders across the country.

COACHES ARE BIG THINKERS

One of the first qualities we see in all great coaches is that they think big. They do their job with one purpose in mind – to develop their players to the point where they are the best they can be so that in the end they all come out winners. Coaches think big. Their objective is to take first place, to win the Super Bowl, to win the World Series, to grab the first place trophy at the end of the season. Losing isn't an option. Have you ever met a coach who said the objective of our season is to come in second place? No, great coaches don't think that way! Maybe your little league coach said that, but no great coach in the NFL, NBA, or MLB is satisfied with second place. Second place, in a great coach's mind, is a useless thought.

Donald Trump once said, "If you're going to be thinking, you might as well think big." That's what great coaches do. They think big. They have the courage to see the big picture, and they go for it. They possess a larger-than-life attitude, and they feel that nothing can stop them from accomplishing their goal.

After all, who in their right mind gets excited about puny ideas, or small dreams? No one does. If a leader doesn't think big or dream big, there's nothing for the leader or his team to get excited about.

Tom Clancy once remarked, "The ultimate defense against growing old is your dream. Nothing is as real as a dream. Your dream is the path between the person you are and the person you hope to become. Success isn't money. Success isn't power. The criteria for your success are to be found in your dream, in yourself. Your dream is something to hold on to. It will always be your link with the person you are today."

The same is true about the dream you have for your team. Your dream, when acted upon, will begin to shape your team into what it needs to be. And, it will begin to take shape the moment you think big.

GODDARD'S MAGIC LIST

It was a rainy day in 1940 when fifteen-year old John, being bored with nothing to do, decided to sit down in his room and write a list of things he'd like to accomplish in his lifetime. After several hours of thoughtful writing, John finally concluded his list of goals. He listed an amazing 127 things he'd like to accomplish during his lifetime. At first, his list started with the simple things that most fifteen year old boys would like to do, such as high jump five feet, long jump fifteen feet, do 200 sit-ups, and weigh 175 pounds. But, then his list went on to include some outlandish goals, such as explore the Nile, fly in a blimp, ride an ostrich, climb the Matterhorn, canoe the Congo, become a writer and a lecturer, visit every country on earth, and visit the moon (his 125th goal)! Believe it or not, this determined young man went on to accomplish 108 of his 127 goals. His name is John Goddard, one of the most inspiring dreamers of our generation.

Someone once asked Goddard how he did it, how he accomplished so much with his life. His answer was that he wasn't afraid to dream big and to make a list, a magical list that reminded him of what he wanted to do with his life. From that magical list, Dr. John Goddard went on to become one of the world's most famous explorers and adventurers. He led the first expedition in history to explore the entire length of the world's longest river, the 4,200-mile Nile River, which the Los Angeles Times called "the most remarkable adventure of this generation." Later, Goddard matched his Nile feat by becoming the first man to explore the entire length of Africa's 2,700-mile Congo River. He has also climbed the lofty peaks in Africa, South America and Asia, including 22,000-foot Huascaran, the highest mountain in the Peruvian Andes, and the 19,000-foot Mt. Kilimanjaro in Tanzania. Dr. Goddard has also been the subject of numerous articles in magazines such as *National Geographic*, *LIFE*, and Reader's Digest, and has been a guest on over 200 television shows, including *"This Is Your Life,"* and NBC's *DATELINE* on April 7, 1998.

What makes Dr. John Goddard one of the most fascinating men of our time? Simply put, his ability to dream! He had big dreams, and although each of them was a tremendous challenge for him to conquer, he conquered them nonetheless. Goddard put it well when he said, "If you really know what you want out of life, it's amazing how opportunities will come to enable some far out goals."

Perhaps as a leader, you're a little discouraged with your team, and it's hard for you to see the big picture under your current circumstances. My advice to you would be to follow the advice of Harper Lee, "Real courage is when you know you're licked before you begin, but you begin anyway and see it through no matter what."

As football coach Paul (Bear) Bryant once said, "If you believe in yourself, have dedication and pride, and never quit, you will always be a winner."

COACHES REACH FOR THE IMPOSSIBLE

In Lewis Carroll's classic book, *Through The Looking Glass*, Carroll writes something very interesting. Although it is a fictional conversation, the theme behind it is very real, and I believe it's something that all leaders should remember. It's okay to have "impossible dreams." The conversation goes like this:

"One can't believe impossible things," said Alice.

"I daresay you haven't had much practice," said the Queen. "When I was your age, I always did it for half-an-hour a day. Why, sometimes I've believed as many as six impossible things before breakfast!"

Dreaming big often means becoming a nonconformist. One such dreamer and nonconformist was the famous philanthropist Jonas Hanway of London, who in the year 1750 was often jeered at for his nonconformist ways. What was his offense? He was the first man to carry an umbrella.

Like the old military saying, I believe there are three types of leaders: Those that make things happen; those who watch things happen; and those who wonder what happened! All great coaches make things happen. They just do. Instead of just thinking about where they are, they also think of where they want to be.

COACHES KEEP GOING NO MATTER WHAT

Great coaches don't let obstacles get them down or get in their way. One of the ways you can measure the greatness of a leader is by what it takes to discourage him or her. Though great leaders aren't immune to discouragement, they've simply learned to keep moving on.

In junior high, I remember going out for track for the first time. I knew I had good speed, but I didn't have a clue as to which event would be the best for me. It wasn't until the coach shared with us boys that he was looking for a few guys to run the hurdles that I became interested. At first glance, they did look a little frightening to me, just sitting out there like a white gate ready to stop me once I tried to maneuver myself over the top of it.

The first thing our coach had us do was to make an attempt to run over them. We all made our humble effort, but it looked more like a running stag leap. Instead of running over the top of them, we leaped as high as we could. Boy, was it ugly!

It wasn't until later that we learned the proper way of running the hurdles. The idea behind successfully running the hurdles is that you are to run through the hurdle, barely clearing the top of it, without any hesitation in your stride. It took six years for me to get it down to perfection. But I did. Eventually, I was able to win district in the hurdles and place in the top ten in state of Missouri.

The lesson I learned from the hurdles is that when you have a hurdle in life or business, just run through it. Keep your eyes focused on the finish line - whatever that may be for you - and don't lose stride.

One day while reading Jack Canfield's and Mark Victor Hansen's first book in their highly popular series, *Chicken Soup For The Soul*, I was amazed at how many of the great stars of the 20th century had obstacles they had to run through to become the great individuals we know them as today.

For example, after legendary actor Fred Astaire's first screen test, a 1933 memo from the MGM Testing Director said: "Can't act. Slightly bald. Can dance a little." When you look back in history you'll find that Fred Astaire didn't let that memo stop him. He ran through it! Eventually, he became world famous as he entertained millions of people on television through his fabulous ability to dance and sing. Astaire kept that memo over his fireplace in his Beverly Hills home.

One day a football expert said of the famous football coach Vince Lombardi: "He possesses minimal football knowledge. Lacks motivation." Yet, Vince Lombardi brushed it off like all great coaches do. Over the years, he has arguably become one of the greatest football coaches of all time. His ability to teach, motivate and inspire players helped turn the Green Bay Packers into the most dominating NFL team in the 1960s, leading them to five NFL Championships, including victories in Super Bowl I and II.

Beethoven handled the violin awkwardly and preferred playing his own compositions instead of improving his technique.

His teacher called him "hopeless" as a composer. But, this didn't stop one of the world's greatest composers.

The voice teacher of the famous opera singer Enrico Caruso said that Caruso "had no voice at all" and could not sing. Despite his teacher's harsh words, Caruso sang to great acclaim at the world's major opera houses.

Walt Disney was fired by a newspaper for lacking good ideas. He also experienced bankruptcy several times. These events didn't stop him from producing some of the world's best known animated films, not to mention creating Disneyland.

Some of the most famous people in the world would have never been famous if they would have let some setback stop them from seeing their dreams to fruition. Each of the people I've mentioned traveled the road of failure before they struck gold. You need to follow the advice of Charles Kettering when he said, "Keep on going, and the chances are that you will stumble onto something, perhaps when you are least expecting it. I have never heard of anyone stumbling on something while sitting down."

If you experience a blow, a setback, a tragedy, and nothing seems to be working, don't stop moving. Keep moving forward! Sitting down and sulking about it doesn't do any good. You can't get anywhere sitting down.

Thomas Watson announced, "Would you like me to give you a formula for success? It's quite simple, really. Double your rate of failure. You're thinking of failure as the enemy of success. But it isn't at all. You can be discouraged by failure - or you can learn from it. So go ahead and make mistakes. Make all you can. Because remember, that's where you'll find success – on the far side of failure."

COACHES COMMUNICATE WELL

Another thing great coaches do is to constantly communicate the game plan. They've learned to become communication experts. They believe in making sure everybody knows what the game plan is. They have a game plan for the whole team, and also a game plan for every individual on the team. And, once the game plan is drawn up, they continually communicate the plan to the team.

The first thing a game-plan coach does is to communicate with the team, as well as with each individual on the team what is expected of them. This not only tells them how they fit into the game plan but also what they should attempt to do. A game-plan coach never tells them "how" to do it, as much as "what" they should do. All too often, an over-eager leader will communicate expectations to the point where they are sounding dictatorial or as a micromanager. And, no one likes a micro-manager.

COACHES ARE FACILITATORS, NOT DICTATORS

The greatest environment of support is created when coaches decide to be facilitators rather than dictators. Total control by the coach, even if he or she is somehow able to achieve it, is never as effective as giving people the opportunity of doing it on their own with the freedom to fail.

Defense Secretary Colin Powell said, "In the military, we always give our recruits the freedom to fail."

Notice the difference between being a dictator and a game-plan coach:

- Dictators make all the decisions, but coaches push the decisions down the line in order to help build future decision-makers. They involve others as much as possible in key decisions and give people space to make those decisions.

- Dictators view themselves as the bearer of truth and wisdom for the team since they are the leader of the group. But coaches view truth and wisdom as something accessible to and present within everyone throughout the team and organization. There is a collective genius and varying perspectives that comes together when you add more people to the discussion.

- Dictators push workers, but coaches empower workers, provide them a vision, and keep them motivated about their work.

- Dictators tend to micro-manage workers with commands from above, but coaches allow their team members to be responsible in deciding how the job is to be done.

- Dictators hold onto power and maintain absolute control, but coaches release power to the team. They are secure in who they are and in their position. They do not fear releasing responsibility to the team.

- Dictators believe they own the team and the job, but coaches encourage the team to find ownership in what they do. They also encourage team participation and creativity.

- Dictators guard their own interests, but coaches serve everyone else's interest by developing people.

- Dictators take for themselves, but coaches give to the organization.

Great coaches understand the level of ability of each team member. One of the most common mistakes a coach can make is to be ignorant of the capabilities of one or all of the team members. Another mistake would be to misjudge the level of one of his players. If the leader doesn't work with each player according to where he or she is in their development, the player won't produce, succeed, or even develop. You must get to know your team, and that means communication.

In his book, *Success Is a Choice*, college basketball coach Rick Pitino tells this story about building a winning team where all players are working on all cylinders, like a well-oiled engine. "When I became the coach of Providence College in the spring of 1985, I was inheriting a program that had been languishing near the bottom of the Big East Conference. In one of my first meetings with the team, I listed four categories on the blackboard: basketball, school, work ethic, and family. The four supposedly most important parts of my new players' lives. 'How many of you want to be professional basketball players someday?' I asked. Virtually every hand in the room went up. 'Well, since you had a losing season last year and no one in this room averaged at least ten points a game, it's obvious you are not a success in the basketball part of your lives.' I said, erasing one quarter of the blackboard. 'And since I've seen your grade-point averages, it's also obvious you aren't successful in school either.' The room was silent as I erased another quarter of the blackboard. Then I asked the trainer how many players had been in the gym every day since the season ended to work on their games.

'No one, Coach,' the trainer said.

'So it's obvious you don't work hard either,' I said, erasing another quarter of the blackboard.

Then I started raising my voice. 'Let's see,' I said. 'You aren't successful in basketball; you aren't successful in school, and you don't work hard. What's left?' I paused for emphasis. 'Well, hopefully, you're a close team,' I finally said. 'Hopefully, you care about each other.'

'Oh, we do, Coach,' said a player named Harold Starks. 'We're a close team.' I pretended to think for a minute.

'Ok, Harold, how many brothers does Steve Wright have?' Starks slowly shook his head. 'What does Billy Donovan's father do for a living?' Harold now looked like a deer stuck in headlights.

'So you really don't know anything about each other, do you?' I asked. No one spoke.

I then made each player stand up and talk about himself and his family. Then something wonderful happened. What had been twelve individuals suddenly had become a cohesive unit, the makings of a team. Twenty-two months later that collection of individuals–now a team–would be in the Final Four Championships.''

Never underestimate the enormous value of communicating with your team. Getting to know them is a critical component to developing team community.

COACHES' FOUR LEVELS OF DEVELOPMENT

According to a research study, *Situation Leadership II Model*, by team management consultant Ken Blanchard, all team members fit into one of four categories with regard to the type of help they need from the leader.

1) The first category consists of team members who need some type of direction. They don't really know what to do or how to do it. At this stage, you need to instruct them nearly every step of the way. Anything these rookie players produce will be essentially what you do through them because they aren't capable of working independently yet.

2) The second category consists of team members who need coaching. At this point, they are able to do more of the job on their own. They are a little bit more independent, but they still rely on you for direction and feedback.

3) The third category consists of team members who need support. Your team member is capable of working without the aid of your direction, but they still rely on your support and encouragement.

4) The fourth category consists of team members to whom you frequently delegate activities. You can be confident they have the competence and know-how to get the job done. These people only need you to lead them. You provide the vision on the front end and accountability on the back end, and the team member will multiply your efforts toward success.

COACHES DEVELOP LEADERS

Great coaches develop team members into leaders. The bottom line is that you can't do it alone. If you really want to be a successful leader, you must realize the importance in developing key leadership within your team.

Most leaders believe that the key to getting things done is to simply put more followers around them. Unfortunately, very few leaders have the knowledge or even take the initiative to surround themselves with other leaders or even go so far as to develop the ones within their group who have the potential. There is no doubt in my mind that the ones who develop their team members into leaders will add great value to their organization. To me, it's the smartest thing a leader can do. You will not only lighten up your load but will have committed help in achieving your vision.

Stop for a moment and think of the people on your team. Are you developing them? Do you have a game plan for them? Are they growing? Have they been able to lift your load? If not, take the time within the next few weeks to develop a game plan for developing leadership within the group. Develop the game plan with the idea that you're going to multiply yourself and create a leader or two or three that will have the capability of replacing you someday.

COACHES SELECT THE RIGHT PLAYERS

When I was pastor of a fast growing church in the south Kansas City area, our church seemed to attract a lot of professionals. One of those professionals was Danan Hughes, one of the great wide receivers for the Kansas City Chiefs football team. I'll never forget the talks Danan and I had regarding the fine-tuned efforts of coaches and scouts selecting the right players for the team. Every year, coaches and owners of professional football teams look forward to the draft allowing their franchises to spend a lot of time and energy scouting out new prospects. These coaches and team owners know the future success of their organization depends largely on their ability to draft effectively.

Today, as a businessman, I realize that it's no different in business than it is in professional sports. In order for a team to be successful, you must select the right players for the organization. If you select well, the benefits are multiplied and endless. If you select poorly, the problems are also multiplied and endless.

In November of 1994, my wife and I felt the leading of God to start a new church in our hometown of Lee's Summit, an exciting and growing suburb of the Kansas City area. We were excited and nervous at the same time.

Lee's Summit had several good churches. It was labeled as the fastest-growing community in Missouri the previous three years. After a lot of prayer, we secured a few families who wanted to join with us and we started the church. We really didn't have a clue about how to start a church, we just knew in our hearts we were supposed to start one.

With no place to meet, my wife agreed that we should clear all of the furniture out of our living room and set up collapsible chairs. We got busy purchasing chairs and stashed all of our living room furniture downstairs in the basement. We also decided to use our bedroom as the children's nursery. As I look back on it now, I feel so proud of my wife and her willingness to allow her home to become something she never planned on or imagined.

Sunday after Sunday, our small group of families brought new people to our home. As we grew, we started to become afraid of what the neighbors would say with all of the cars parked out in front and lining down the street. After three months, we finally felt compelled to find a larger place.

We moved our church to the conference room at a local hotel and started to advertise for the first time. For the next consecutive three months, we continued to experience good growth and, once again, felt compelled to find yet another larger location.

Within six months of starting the church, we ended up purchasing a small church building in town. A year later, on our first year anniversary, we had packed out the church with nearly 300 people attending. We were excited and having fun!

The fun continued for four years, until a personal tragedy took place. The honeymoon was over. A fast growing church can outgrow the facility and parking capacity, which can cause a church to stagnate, and even go backwards in attendance. Thinking about all of these things robbed me of the joy of pastoring. The church was too full. It was a good problem to have, but everyone felt the pressure to find something larger and more efficient for our new ministries. As all of this was building up, a couple of serious tragedies took place at the same time. Two of our most precious members died, one from cancer and the other from a supposed suicide.

With all of this going on, it seemed like my life was spinning out of control. I was allowing myself to become overwhelmed with the heart-wrenching challenges that faced me. It affected me to the point that I was getting ill and becoming prone to stress-induced anxiety. I felt like the walls of the church were caving in on me. In addition, I felt my relationship with my family becoming strained. Somehow, the pressures and expectations in keeping up with a fast-growing church started to creep up on me and seemed to put a tight strangle-hold on my life, mentally, physically, and spiritually.

One thing I've learned from that experience is *you can do many righteous things, but not necessarily the right things.* I was actively involved in so many things: pastoring, counseling, working on my master's degree, writing my first book, developing our discipleship course, hosting a weekly radio broadcast, serving as the senior chaplain of our local police department, and planning for the building of a new church facility. I did a lot of good things, but it spread me so thin that I wasn't able to concentrate on just doing the right things – the things essentials to nurturing a growing church. Eventually, I ended up at the doctor's office one morning, physically shaken from a panic attack. I had never experienced depression or anxiety attacks before, but now I knew something was wrong.

At my request, the leaders of the church agreed that I needed some time off. I took a few days off and headed to Colorado where I could get alone with my thoughts and God. After three days of serious introspection and reflection, I believed that the best thing for me to do at that time under my current physical and mental condition was to resign and turn over my leadership to another individual, a very capable man that I had been mentoring for a few years.

Without hesitation, my friend and fellow co-laborer, Phil took the mantle of leadership. Phil was a highly decorated police sergeant in the metro division of the Kansas City Police Department. He had leadership skills that just leaked out.

- He could think clearly in a crisis.

- He would listen intently before speaking out.

- He had ample experience in delegating effectively.

- His team of fellow officers under his leadership were proud to serve with him.

- He had the motivation to do what was needed to be done without being asked.

These were just a few of the many qualities I could see in Phil. So, when he first mentioned to me that he wanted to leave the police force and become a pastor of a church, I immediately began delegating some church leadership responsibilities to him.

- I invited him to join the church board to gain experience at what goes on at that level.

- I let him take over as the teacher of my adult Sunday school class so that he could work on his speaking and teaching skills.

- I let him teach the entire church in my absence on Sunday's when I was sick or couldn't be there.

- I also took him on mission trips into Mexico so that we could talk, get to know each other more intimately, and so he could learn more about the expectations involved in being a pastor.

Since that time, Phil has done an incredible job in growing and nurturing the people of the church. In fact, under his brilliant leadership, the church has been steadily growing, breaking new attendance records every year.

Fortunately for me, I had the opportunity of mentoring a very teachable and likeable maverick.

As I look back on my time with Phil, I realize how important it is for leaders to work themselves out of a job. I did my job. I started the church and lead it to a point where one of my disciples could nurture it to even greater heights of ministry.

A number of people have asked me over the years, "Do you regret resigning as the pastor of Abundant Life Baptist Church?" My answer to them is always the same, "No!" I've never once felt the regret of leaving. My job was to start the church, and that's what I did. Since that time, the church has taken a giant leap forward with more than 5,000 people attending every Sunday morning as of this writing. This is exactly what effective, peak performance leadership is all about. It's about leading and developing leaders who can take the mantle of responsibility after you're gone. What a legacy that leaves!

Every time I drive by the large, new church buildings that comprise nearly half a city block, I'm thrilled I invested my knowledge and time with Phil. I'm thankful for taking him on mission trips, allowing him to teach my adult class, instilling within him the vision of our church, and becoming a close personal friend. Each time I see him, he shares with me how he's still carrying on with the initial vision of the church. However, I'm sure that vision has expanded to greater heights that I ever dreamed of. I'm excited about that, and it gives me the greatest feeling of accomplishment knowing that I took the time to invest myself in helping to build a potential leader.

Though Phil already had the right stuff that makes an excellent leader, God simply used me to pave the path towards him becoming a more effective leader, a leader within our church - and now a pastor who is mentoring numerous other pastors throughout the country.

When initially scouting out potential leaders that you would like to invest yourself into, I would recommend that you begin with the DATA principle. Here's an acrostic of what I mean:

D-Desire: Does the individual have the desire to be highly successful?

A-Abilities: Does the individual have the ten basic skills necessary to lead? A good reader, writing skills, speaking skills, computer skills, listening skills, problem-solving capabilities, self-control, competence, a team player?

T-Temperament: Does the individual have the social skills to effectively deal with customers, coworkers, and managers?

A-Assets: Does the individual have that "extra something" that others don't have?

To add to the list, here are few more characteristics Maxwell says that leaders need to look for in an individual who carries the traits of an effective future leader:

- **Positivity** - the ability to work with and see people and situations in a positive way.

- **Servitude** - the willingness to submit, plays team ball and follows the leader.

- **Growth Potential** - a hunger for personal growth and development.

- **Follow-Through** - the determination to get the job done efficiently.

- **Loyalty** - the willingness to always put the leader and the organization above personal desires.

- **Resiliency** - the ability to bounce back when problems arise.

- **Integrity** - a trustworthy and solid character.

- **Big-Picture Mindset** - the ability to see the big picture.

- **Discipline** - the willingness to do what is required regardless of personal mood.

- **Gratitude** - an attitude of thankfulness that's a way of life.

Once you've identified the potential leaders within your team, you'll need to begin the work of building them into the leaders they can become. To do this, you'll need a strategy.

COACHES OFFER TIME AND TRAINING

First of all, you'll want to offer them your personal time. People cannot be nurtured from a distance or by infrequent short spurts of attention. They need you to spend time with them, planned time, not just a few words on the way to a meeting. Unfortunately, time is a precious commodity to the leader of a team, but nurturing leaders must maintain a giving attitude when it comes to their time. As Norman Vincent Peale once said, "A man who lives for himself is a failure; the man who lives for others has achieved true success."

Secondly, you'll want to extend to them some kind of sufficient training. Recently, I read an article written by Richard Wellins, William Byham, and Jeanne Wilson detailing a list of things that experts have concluded are the six biggest factors, which "inhibit" a team-building environment. Of the six, the first was "insufficient training." The unfortunate thing about a lot of organizations is that they see little value in the time spent training an individual effectively.

As someone who has trained managers and supervisors in seminars in three countries, I've seen firsthand how the process of training can dramatically improve the quality of an individual and enhance their work performance. The danger zone for many leaders is in the field of assumption. Many leaders automatically assume people have certain skills or knowledge. To assume is dangerous and can be catastrophic.

I remember speaking to a group of managers and supervisors at a hotel convention center in Grand Rapids, Michigan, a few years ago. During the break, a sharp, intelligent-looking gentleman named Richard came up to me with a perplexed look on his face. He was the head of his engineering team at a large architectural firm in the city and was having some problems dealing with an individual on his team. He told me he was going to have to leave the seminar early to deal with the guy on some unrelenting issues. He said he would be back later that afternoon. However, before he left for the office, he thought he'd ask me for some advice. He explained to me that this certain person had quite the dominating personality and he didn't know how to handle him.

Since I had just finished a three-hour session on how to deal with the different personality types almost all teams have, I told him to simply look over his notes and apply the information to that type of personality. He agreed that he would give it a try and left. About two hours later, he came back into the room with a huge smile on his face. At the next break, he told me what had happened and how the training was exactly what he needed to deal with this certain person on his team.

About a year later, his company, an internationally recognized engineering firm, invited me to speak to all the team leaders on the different personality traits and how to deal with them. I, once again, had the opportunity to speak with Richard, and I was glad to hear that he was still doing well in his working relationship with the former "problem" employee. Training does make a difference when it comes to being effective in dealing with other people.

A number of years ago, I had the privilege of visiting the fastest growing organization in Topeka, Kansas. Their leader was a brilliant coach. He was able to take them from an organization of about 20 people to more than 100 individuals across five different departments, all of which were doing a splendid job of training insurance agents and financial planners on how to make more money in their business. Scores of agents were calling them up and flying out to their highly informative training sessions every week. What made them so unique as an organization was their ability to train people to become better at what they do. They were masters at it.

Not only did they provide training for thousands of financial professionals, but they were also committed to providing training to their employees every day. With every new day, their employees woke up, went to work, and entered first and foremost into a training session. Each day, at 8:30 in the morning, they trained their staff on how to be more effective in helping life insurance agents and financial professionals find the right product for their clients. From the people at the switchboard to the team leaders within each department, they were all uniquely trained to do their job and to do it better than anyone else in the business. To walk around the entire organization and to talk with the young staff of people that day was exhilarating. They were a young, vibrant, professional, and committed team of people who made good money, got three weeks' vacation each year, had great benefits, and most of all, they had a leader who was a fabulous coach. He had become their hero. His commitment to building success in everyone on his team was the key to getting his team to happily follow his lead!

COACHES ADDRESS PROBLEMS EARLY

Great coaches effectively deal with problems on the team. Problems are a part of life and work. Every company and organization will experience problems – plenty of them! Moreover, they are a part of every team. Let's face it, as a leader you are going to encounter problems. Problems are as natural as breathing. As someone once said, "If death and taxes are the first two certainties of life, conflict is the third." But how you deal with the kind of conflicts and problems the team encounters will make all the difference in the world.

The first thing to realize about problem solving is that problems are necessary. It's not necessarily a bad thing to have problems. Problems can be a good thing for an organization. In fact, it's healthy to have a few. It's only when you have too many problems and they're out of control—that's when problems become a bad thing.

I remember a problem that I had to confront when I started pastoring the new church. One of the biggest mistakes a leader could make is to look past a problem or try to avoid confronting it. All went well for the first four years. We experienced no complaints or problems from anyone. After the fourth year, our first complaint arrived. I learned there were families who didn't agree on how we ran our church business meetings. Sadly, I minimized the problem. I avoided it. I thought, *"Hey, these people love the church, it can't be that big of a problem for them."* Boy, was I wrong! It was a big problem for them. Eventually, they became more upset and started sharing their problem with other people within the church. The next time we had a business meeting, I learned just how many people they had talked to. By now, it seemed like there were five or six families who were a little agitated with the business meeting.

This problem started to spread. I finally made an effort to take the problem seriously enough to confront those families. Eventually, we were able to resolve the issues to a satisfactory agreement. Unfortunately, for me and the church, because I did not take the initiative to resolve the issue as soon as it came up, the other four or five families became involved. Fortunately, it all worked out. I got a good glimpse of how ugly things can get if you wait too long to solve a problem.

The one primary thing all leaders need to do is to address problems early on. You need to head them off quickly. It will save you a world of heartache and future troubles.

One day while chatting with a friend of mine named Mike, who served as the associate pastor of one of the most dynamic churches in south Florida, I found they were growing by leaps and bounds, and the church's health was off the charts. While on the phone I asked him, "What do you feel is the reason for the church's great health?"

The first thing Mike mentioned to me was that his pastor had the unique quality of dealing with problems before they get out of hand. He wasn't afraid to address the issues at stake because he cared so much for the rest of church congregation. By taking the initiative to be out and about, listening to his people, and dealing with every concern his people had, this pastor was able to lead this church to becoming one of the most stable, growing churches in south Florida.

The first instinct of most leaders is to respond defensively. This is always the worst response. When dealing with conflict, a leader should never confront problems with a defensive attitude. Instead, they should have a solution attitude. A defensive attitude can easily be recognized and felt. In the very beginning, it tends to polarize the issue into sides, for and against. Remember, if you're going to solve the problem, you're going to be dealing with three keys things: a person's pride, personality, and persuasion.

In the end, someone has to win and someone has to lose; someone has to be right and someone has to be wrong. Since this will be the inevitable outcome, you've got to keep in mind that pride, personality, and persuasion are all part of the resolution process. If the incentive is to win, then there's no learning or growing taking place. The conflict eventually takes on a life of its own, driven by self-protection, saving face and defending reputations. Honest disagreements suddenly become personal attacks. Emotions rise, feeding a cycle of insecurity, distrust, and bitterness. Obviously, this is a leader's nightmare.

Every leader must be the first to own the problem. Though you may not be at fault, the leader still needs to ask the question, "What is it about me that is causing this to happen?" Remember, everything rises and falls with leadership.

But what if you're not involved? You still must to resist the urge to blame, unless it is absolutely mandatory. Assigning blame is one of the greatest obstacles to real learning and resolution. By resisting the urge to blame, you can remove people and events from focus. Then, you'll be able to uncover the underlying issues and correct the patterns of behavior to which the whole team contributes.

George Cheatham, writing in the Association Source of the Florida Society of Association Executives, offers six condensed ways to building a good coaching relationship between you and your team:

1. **Be friendly to team members,** but don't treat them like close personal friends. Separate business from personal

relationships. They want you to be the boss, and they want to be employees. It works better that way.

2. **Tell them everything** and expect them to tell you the same. Shared knowledge builds loyalty and trust.

3. **Practice Pulitzer-Prize plagiarism.** Steal only from the best. If you need help, reach out to your professional community. Someone, somewhere, somehow will know how to help you.

4. **Invest heavily in loyalty.** If staff members know that you're always loyal to them, they'll give you the same in return. According to the Hay Group, after reviewing 75 components of employee satisfaction, they concluded that trust and confidence in top leadership is the single most reliable predictor of employee satisfactions.

5. **Realize that fairness establishes your credibility** as a coach.

6. **Never be too busy to laugh.** Nothing gets people through crisis like a good laugh - and a leader who's willing to enjoy it with them.

Another thing to consider as a leader of people is that regardless of your leadership style, you're an influencer. Everyone is an influencer of people. It doesn't matter who you are or what your occupation is, everyone has an influence on others. The question is, "What kind of an influencer are you?"

As Ralph Waldo Emerson said, "Every man is a hero, and an oracle to somebody and to that person, whatever he says has an enhanced value."

Decide today to become a coach! And, as a coach, you'll need to build your peak performance team by casting the right vision for your team. The next chapter will explain to you how to do just that.

Chapter 4
Building Your Team
Through Vision

Who would have thought one hundred years ago that we'd be where we are today in our world relative to the incredible advancements in both the fields of technology, science, medicine, telecommunications, and space exploration? Probably no one, unless, of course, you were part of a select few who were deep inside these industries sitting alongside those who were fabulous visionaries.

The story is told of the French historian and atheist Voltaire who once criticized the famous scientist Sir Isaac Newton for speculating that one-day men may travel at speeds of 40 miles per hour. With disgust, Voltaire refuted Newton's idea saying, "See what a fool Christianity makes of an otherwise brilliant man! Here is a scientist like Newton who actually writes that men may travel at the rate of 30 or 40 miles per hour. Has he forgotten that if man would travel at this rate he would be suffocated? His heart would stand still!"

Obviously, Voltaire wasn't a visionary. What would Voltaire say if he discovered that some two hundred years after he wrote this comment that an American astronaut, Edward H. White, on June 3, 1965, would climb out of a spacecraft a hundred miles in the sky and casually walk across the continental United States in less than fifteen minutes, strolling along at 17,500 m.p.h.? What would Voltaire think today if he could see our homes surging full of electricity bringing us heat, light, and power to run our modern household appliances or witness thousands of people each day traveling at speeds of 500 m.p.h. in an airplane, crisscrossing the country in a few hours rather than in months or years? What would he think concerning our lifesaving advances in medicine, which have allowed us to control fever, pneumonia, tuberculosis, and other diseases that ravaged our nation in their day? And what jaw-dropping statements would he make of our ability to globalize communications so that we can talk to anyone in the world or view any country in the world by way of telephone, television, the internet, and Google Earth?

All of the modem conveniences we experience today are the by-product of visionaries. They saw it in our future; they dreamed about it as they worked, and they worked hard to help others catch the dream. As others caught the vision, they envisioned the world as better, faster, larger, and more efficient.

With the advent of nanotechnology, we are anticipating a whole, new world. This will be a world where we'll have computer chips in just about everything: our clothes, our bodies, our appliances, our homes, our books, and so on. We'll enter into a complex global brain system that will practically think for us. The picture of our future is a breathtaking one, and it will all take place because someone had vision.

VISION IS NOT AN OPTION

Let's get one thing straight. If you want to be a leader vision is not just an option. It is part of the standard equipment of a real leader. As George Barna once put it, "By definition, a leader has vision. Why else would a leader lead people toward, if not to fulfill that vision?" Leaders are visionary people. They have to be. For the sake of their future and the team, they have to be. It is Leroy Eims who says, "A leader is one who sees more than others see, who sees farther than others see, and who sees before others do."

Even the Bible emphasizes the critical importance of the need for vision. Israel's King Solomon once said, "Where there is no vision, the people perish." – Proverbs 11:20

Unless a leader has a clear understanding of where the team is headed, the probability of a successful journey is severely limited. In the end, everyone loses.

When my children were little, they used to enjoy taking a leisurely Sunday afternoon drive out in the country. Every Sunday, after church, we'd grab something to eat at a local restaurant, then head out into the country. To us, there was nothing more relaxing than driving through beautiful, hilly landscapes on a lazy, sunny afternoon. As we drove for miles, we'd keep ourselves amused with singing songs and playing different games. One of the games we'd play while we were out driving around was to let my kids choose which road they wanted me to take. They loved that part of the drive. Invariably, they would always have me drive down the old, dark, bumpy ones that had the appearance of leading us into nowhere. They amused themselves with the idea that perhaps they could get me lost. Though I would never tell them, at times, it would work.

On one such Sunday afternoon, we had traveled quite some distance over a period of a couple of hours. The sun was bright, and the warmth within the car made everyone sleepy. Eventually, my wife and the children fell asleep. I wanted to, but obviously, I was the designated driver. While weaving down those country roads, I began to think about how much fun we were having going nowhere in specific, just driving. All of sudden it occurred to me that there are many people in life and business that are doing the same thing we were doing-- weaving in and out of the scenic highways and byways without any specific destination in mind. The unfortunate thing is that life is too short and business runs too fast to just take a drive to nowhere. Taking a Sunday afternoon approach to life and business can leave a person feeling unfulfilled and on the short end of their intended expectations.

The purpose of those Sunday afternoon drives for our family was to enjoy being together, to relax while we traveled the roads that led to no particular destination. Our goal was to have fun going nowhere. But in life and business, you can't afford to do that. There needs to be an end in mind, a vision if you will.

Without an end in mind, you end up becoming what motivational expert Zig Ziglar describes as a "wandering generality" instead of a "meaningful specific."

VISION VS. MISSION

Someone once asked me at a leadership conference, "What exactly is vision? Are vision and mission the same?" At first glance, vision and mission appear to be the same. But they are not. Clearly, there is a distinct difference between the two.

A vision statement focuses more about the future of the company. It's a source of inspiration and motivation. It outlines where you ultimately want to go, where you eventually want to be, and the change you want to make in your industry. It may be more general in nature.

A mission statement, however, concentrates more on the present. It defines what you as a company intend to do and how you're going to accomplish the vision. The mission is more specific in nature and is a statement that supports the vision and provides a path towards it.

Let me give you specific examples of what I mean:

- A vision statement shares "where" you want to be or "what" you'll want to become in the future. A mission statement talks about "how" you'll fulfill the vision. It defines the purpose and primary objectives.

- A vision statement answers the question, "What do we aim to be?" It usually never changes. A mission statement answers the question, "How do we intend to get there? Who are we? And, what makes us different from everyone else in our field?"

- A vision statement is broad in nature and inspires you to give your best and helps you to understand "why" you're there. A mission statement is specific in nature and defines your audience, reveals your goals, and shares your core values. A mission statement is more flexible to change as the company approaches the stated vision.

I hope this helps clarify the differences between mission and vision. let's explore vision just a little bit further.

If you were to ask George Barna, a researcher who has written an excellent book about vision, he would describe it as, "a clear, mental image of a preferable future - a picture in your mind's eye of the way things could or should be in the days ahead." That's what it is! It's the ultimate, yet realistic dream of what you'd like your team to become and what you want your team to produce in the future. It includes a reflection of your present circumstances and the changes you'd like to make. It's built on reality, but at the same time, it means dreaming the most possible dream you could dream. It's not about impossibilities, but rather a realistic perspective of the most possible thing you could do.

In their book, *Changing The Essence*, Richard Beckhard and Wendy Pritchard have said, "A vision is a picture of a future state for the organization, a description of what it would like to be a number of years from now. It is a dynamic picture of the organization in the future, as seen by its leadership."

During his 1968 presidential campaign, Senator Robert F. Kennedy once used a brilliant quote by playwright George Bernard Shaw: "Some men see things as they are, and say, why; I dream things that never were and say, why not?"

Let me ask you some hard questions. Do you have a vision statement for your team or organization? You may have a mission statement, but do you have a vision statement as well? Are you or anyone else capable of articulating that statement at any given time? Is it in written format and plastered everywhere so that everyone is reminded of it? Do you promote it regularly in your meetings with the team or casually remind them in conversations? Is your team pumped up about the vision statement and working hard to meet it? Does your team feel a sense of ownership in it? If not, then my suggestion would be to develop one that meets all of these questions with a resounding "yes."

The first thing you want to do in developing the right vision for you and your team is for you to look down the road and dream of future possibilities that you think could be ahead of you. The purpose of vision is not to estimate the future, but to create it. The vision you want to develop will define the parameters within which you and your team's future will emerge. Realize that the future is not something that just happens; it is a reality that is created by those strong enough to exert control over their environment.

The very first thing I do when starting a new venture is to pray about it. I believe that vision is something that is born in the mind of God and transcended to the mind of man. I believe that God's foreknowledge and sovereignty are a part of what goes on in this world and in our lives. Consequently, to me, I think it would be a little naive to not consider what God has to say about it first and foremost.

God also grants wisdom, something you'll need when developing a vision. The Bible says in the Book of James, "If any man lacks wisdom, let him ask of God, who gives to all men liberally, and upbraids not."

Regardless of your faith or whether you believe in praying about it or not, it's important to remember that the future you develop for your team depends largely upon the vision you establish right now. Vision has the power to influence the future, to change it for the better.

In the early 1980's, Howard Schultz went on a coffee-buying trip to Milan, Italy. He was a buyer for Starbucks Coffee Company, which at that time sold coffee beans in five specialty stores in Seattle. However, in Italy, Schultz caught a glimpse of a vision for his future. He noticed in Italy that there were crowds of city dwellers who began each day with a stop in a coffee bar. He wondered, maybe this could happen in America.

Back in Seattle, he petitioned his two bosses to let him start a cafe. They refused. Schultz quit the company in an effort to try out his own idea. He immediately pursued some 200 investors and finally was able to raise $1.7 million. In April 1986, Schultz opened his first cafe in downtown Seattle. It was called Starbucks.

In less than a year, Schultz opened two more cafes, and eventually, he bought out his former bosses for $4 million. By August 1987, Schultz had the Starbucks name over his three cafes, and the rest of his success story has become a tribute to vision. He looked down the road and saw future possibilities and took advantage of them.

You might want to, right now, take a few minutes to think about the most possible dream you could dream for you and your team. What would it be? Don't start viewing all of the negatives and talk yourself out of what could be, just start listing what you'd like them to be.

The right vision for a team can inspire them to do things they would never otherwise attempt. Remember John F. Kennedy's vision to place a man on the moon by the end of the 1960's. It inspired and mobilized a nation to accomplish the seemingly impossible. Martin Luther King Jr.'s "I have a dream" speech on the Lincoln Memorial before some 250,000 people literally electrified his listeners and shook the nation into change. Vision has a way of motivating people.

In his book, *Visionary Leadership*, Burt Nanus writes, "There is no more powerful engine driving an organization toward excellence and long range success than an attractive, worthwhile, achievable vision for the future, widely shared."

The biggest challenge for the leader, however, is coming up with the right vision. Asking people to sacrifice for the sake of puny visions doesn't get people too excited about anything. And lofty vision statements are not enough, either. Though companies might generate a respectable goal of "five percent gain in market share next year" or "ten percent less waste next year," it doesn't always carry with it any obvious personal benefit. Numbers by themselves never excite anyone but an accountant.

Leaders often fail to appeal to people's innate need to believe they have made a valuable contribution to society. If people are going to make sacrifices, they want to know how these sacrifices are going to benefit others as well as themselves. People want to be a part of something significant. People want their lives to make a difference.

THE DREAM FOR THE TEAM

Hans Finzel, in his book *The Top Ten Mistakes Leaders Make*, offers sound advice about the steps a leader might take to develop a vision for him or her and the team. Let me give you a few in the form of questions that you, as a leader, must answer:

1) First, as the leader, what do you see as your team's vision? What is the ultimate intended outcome you'd like to see in your team? Every leader needs to set aside some time to think about the future. Creating vision and direction toward the future is one of the primary tasks of leadership. The leader is responsible to take the lead in planning for the future. I think it's important that every quarter a leader ought to purposefully establish as part of his or her schedule to set aside time to thoughtfully consider the future. If a leader will do this, it will keep him or her creative, determined, and focused.

When you set aside those times, ask yourself what you would like to ultimately accomplish. While developing these thoughts, it's a good idea to bring along a piece of paper and a pen. Be sure to write down your thoughts as they come. Think in terms of three years, five years, or maybe even twenty. If you could choose the most perfect dream of what you'd like your team to become and what you'd like your team to perform, what would that look like? Write it down and ponder it over the next several days or weeks.

2) Does your team have the skills, resources, and ability to fulfill the vision? Secondly, Finzel advises that the leader perform a vision audit. In other words, take the time to ask insiders and outsiders about how they feel about your team, as well as what they see as the strengths and weaknesses of your organization or team. Send out questionnaires seeking the honest feedback of your respondents. Those questions might include:

- What are the strengths of our group?

- What are our greatest weaknesses?

- What should be our highest priorities?

- What do we do well?

- What do we do poorly?

- What barriers do we need to remove to fundamentally enhance our effectiveness as a team?

3) How are you including your team in the development of your vision statement? As you consider the vision for you and your team, plan to invite your team to help you in establishing the vision. This will not only allow you to expand your ideas of what kind of vision should be established for the team, but it gives them buy-in power. This vision will be a part of them. They will have ownership in it.

As you bring your team in on it, remember that vision is not something you create, it's something that is a part of you - you already own it. As Barna puts it, "Vision is not the result of consensus; it should result in consensus."

While developing your vision, it should entail risk. Why? Because it means change. It means that the team will have to undergo a stretching of talent and an openness for developing creativity and improvements. It may mean more training, more tools, more people, less paperwork, a different environment, etc. As the team pushes forward, you must insist on an aggressive effort, because remaining stationary is tantamount to losing ground. Without risk, no progress can be made.

4) How do you and the team specifically plan to accomplish the vision? The next step you'll want to take is to allow your vision to take a form of strategy. It asks the question, "How are we going to accomplish this?" Barna says, "Vision is conceptual, but it also is practical and detailed." He goes on to add, "The detail inherent within strategy is a reflection of a strong vision, one that encompasses a detailed view of what will be in the days ahead."

5) Are you developing your vision with the right words that fully describe the vision you and your team wish to accomplish? Another stage of vision development would include putting together a fresh vision statement. As you and your team work on creating the vision, be sure to write your ideas down as they come. Work on the words that you put down on paper so that you can condense the words into a sentence or phrase that is easily remembered and articulated by all team members.

When developing your vision statement, use the following checks and balances. Take note that powerful and transforming visions always tend to possess the following special properties:

- They are appropriate for the organization and the time.

- They set standards of excellence and reflect high ideals.

- They clarify purpose and direction.

- They inspire enthusiasm and encourage commitment.

- They are well articulated and easily understood.

- They reflect the uniqueness of the organization.

- They are ambitious.

Your vision statement should be spelled out in a few words in order for your team to memorize it and be able to articulate it at any time. Having your team able to articulate the vision at any time is critical. To do this, you'll need your team to help you. It needs to be clear to them. It not only aids in providing them buy-in power, but it also gives them a feeling of ownership. They realize this is not your vision, but the vision of the entire team. It's not about you; it's about them.

6) Does your vision statement meet the criteria of the SMART principle? Another thing you'll want to do is to get together with your team to develop short-term and long-term strategic goals. You've considered the end result, now how are you going to get there?

As you put together these goals, be sure to follow the SMART principle.

S - Specific: Your goals must be specific.

M - Measurable: Your goals must be able to be measured.

A - Achievable: Are your goals truly achievable? Are they realistic?

R - Relevant: How relevant are the goals to reaching your vision?

T - Timed: You must be able to track your goals based on a timetable.

It's important that these goals are flexible, and involve at least a two-level process. The first process would involve annual goals, and the second process would involve quarterly goals.

7) How will you advertise your vision and keep it in front of everyone so that it soaks into your team members' minds and hearts? The next stage in developing a fresh vision for the team would be to advertise it. Place it everywhere! Remember, if it's out of sight, it's out of mind.

Leaders need to realize that takes some time for the team members to absorb a vision, too. Thomas Smith, a nineteenth century London businessman, offered the following advice to advertisers in 1885. He comments on the time it takes for people to absorb any type of advertisement information and find the value of buying into it. Though he speaks primarily of an advertisement to buy a product, your vision still must receive buy-in from your team. Your team is your customer. You'll need to sell the concept of the vision and keep it in front of them at all times. Here's what he said:

The first time people look at any given ad, they don't even see it.

The second time, they don't notice it.

The third time, they are aware that it is there.

The fourth time, they have a fleeting sense that they've seen it somewhere before.

The fifth time, they actually read the ad.

The sixth time, they thumb their nose at it.

The seventh time, they start to get a little irritated with it.

The eighth time, they start to think, "Here's that ad again."

The ninth time, they start to wonder if they may be missing out on something.

The tenth time, they ask their friends and neighbors if they've tried it.

The eleventh time, they wonder how the company is paying for all these ads.

The twelfth time, they start to think that it must be a good idea.

The thirteenth time, they start to feel it has value.

The fourteenth time, they start to realize they've wanted it for a long time.

The fifteenth time, they start to really want it.

The sixteenth time, they accept that they will buy into it sometime in the future.

The seventeenth time, they make a note of it to buy into it.

The eighteenth time, they think it's terrific.

The nineteenth time, they count their money carefully in order to buy it.

The twentieth time, they buy into what it is offering.

Smith is telling us that it takes time to sell someone. It also takes a consistent and repetitive form of advertisement. It takes keeping it in front of your team members at all times. That old adage rings true—out of sight, out of mind.

One of the reasons, I believe the Amway Corporation is so successful with their distributors is that they continually encourage people to come to their meetings. They know that if their distributors are encouraged to keep their eyes on their financial goals, they'll more than likely reach them someday. In fact, one of the internal motivating factors they encourage their distributors to do is to put a picture of their goal on their refrigerator. That way, every day, they'll see their goal and find the inner motivation to keep treading the difficult waters of doing business and fight off the waves of discouragement and doubt.

If your desire is to build and train a peak performance team, plan on it, dream on it, commit to it and take an iron-grit determination to make it happen. Write it down so that you can review it often.

This reminds me of a university study conducted years ago about the importance in writing your goals down and keeping them where you have the opportunity to review them often. In the study, they reviewed the students of one particular graduating class. They found that the students who had written down goals at graduation went on to collectively do far more than the rest of the class who didn't. The university study proves the old adage, "Out of sight, out of mind."

So, write down your goals. Keep them in front of you at all times. And go for it!

Chapter 5
Empowering a
Peak Performance Team

A great example of a peak performance team that many people can identify with is the talented team at the NASA Space Center in Houston, Texas. These highly trained, technical experts from various fields have learned to network on a rare level. Together, they accomplished one of the world's greatest feats: sending a human being into space 22 times faster than a speeding bullet and bringing them safely back to earth. For NASA, there has perhaps never been a more remarkable display of peak performance ability than what millions of people around the world witnessed during the failed Apollo 13 Mission.

During the 1960's and 1970's, America was in a space race with Russia and the Apollo 13 operation was to be the third American moon mission. At 2:13 EST on April 11, 1970, Mission Commander, James A. Lovell; Command Module Pilot, John L. Swigert, Jr.; and Lunar Module Pilot Fred W. Haise blasted off from Pad 39A at Cape Canaveral heading into space at an incredible speed.

Outside of a short S-11 engine burn, the Apollo 13 space mission was virtually flawless. In fact, at 46 hours 43 minutes Joe Kerwin, the CapCom on duty, said, "The spacecraft is in real good shape as far as we are concerned. We're bored to tears down here." It was the last time anyone would mention boredom for a long time.

Fifty-five hours into the mission, the crew began a television transmission from the command module to the rest of the world. During this time, Fred Haise and Jim Lovell showed the depleting television audience the effects of weightlessness in space, all of this going on to the musical tune of "Aquarius" and "Hair."

Fifty-six hours into the flight, Mission Control asked Swigert to stir cryogenic oxygen tanks one and two. As the power fans turned on within the tank, the exposed fan wires shorted and the Teflon insulation caught fire. This fire spread along the wires to the electrical conduit on the side of the tank, which weakened and ruptured under the nominal 1000 psi within, causing the number two oxygen tank to explode. As a result, this damaged the number one tank and several parts of the interior of the service module. Consequently, bay cover number four blew completely off. A loud bang reverberated throughout the spacecraft. Warning lights went off everywhere inside the module. Swigert reported the frightening news back to earth, "Okay, Houston, hey, we've got a problem here."

For two seconds Mission Control lost telemetry. With each second ticking, the spacecraft was losing precious oxygen, water, and electricity. Without oxygen, the astronauts would obviously suffocate. Without electricity, the astronauts would freeze to death in frigid space.

As news of the astronaut's plight hit the news agencies around the world, the whole world stood in awe realizing the dreadful truth. These three astronauts were in grave danger. What was once termed a "boring flight" now gained unprecedented prime time coverage and interest worldwide. All eyes were fixed on the fate of these three brave, young astronauts. Prayer vigils started worldwide, and foreign countries offered their services for a recovery. At the manned space flight centers, concern filled the room, matched by a determination to do whatever was necessary to return the astronauts safely to earth.

What happened next was nothing short of peak performance. Mission Control director, Gene Krantz, and the men and women of the Black Team, Gold Team, White Team, and Maroon Team performed the impossible. As Gene Krantz put it, "Failure is not an option!" These men and women pulled together in one of the most fascinating and remarkable feats human beings have been called to perform. With the help of Ken Mattingly (who was supposed to be on the flight but was released due to a misdiagnosis of German Measles by the flight doctor), these incredible people brought these three stranded astronauts back safely to earth.

After a flight time of 142 hours and 54 minutes, Apollo 13 splashed down in the Pacific Ocean on April 17, 1970, and 1:07 EST. Since then, it has been called "The most successful failure" in space exploration history. If it were not for the dynamic results in the team at NASA working as a peak performance team, the results would have been different. Without the powerful combination of a committed flow of communication and dependence on each team being uniquely empowered to do their job, the unfortunate may have occurred.

Fortunately for NASA, they had several teams who had been trained and empowered to do their complicated job and to do it well.

SETTING YOUR TEAM UP FOR SUCCESS

When I speak of empowerment, I mean the capability of your team to do their job and do it well. When your team members are empowered to work to their fullest capability, it means that you, as a leader, have provided them the necessary resources to succeed. It means that you have set them up for success from the very beginning. If they need the right equipment to succeed, it means you've gone to whatever lengths necessary to get them what they need. If it's training that's required, then you're doing what you can to provide them the training they need. Empowerment is one of the most critical factors in developing a peak performance team.

When I discuss empowerment in this chapter, I want to talk primarily about the subjects of delegation and communication. From my experience as a corporate trainer, these two subject matters seem to be of the greatest concerns among managers and supervisors.

DELEGATE OR STAGNATE

Delegation is simply the act of "entrusting something to someone else." It sounds so simple, but most people never fully realize their potential in life simply because they never learn how to delegate things to others.

Several years ago when our children were going through their teenage years, our house could easily get rearranged, as you can imagine. There were always clothes to be picked up, rooms to clean, laundry to be done, dishes to be washed, meals to be made, and a wide assortment of other things I won't take the time to labor on, simply because it stresses me out to think about it.

My wife and I both grew up in homes that strongly encouraged us to keep things around the house nice and clean. My wife, however, is quite the perfectionist. I do not mean that in a negative way at all. In fact, I adore the fact that she keeps our home looking like a showroom. Unfortunately for her, when she came home from a hard day's work, she felt compelled to a clean and organize everything our children decided to rearrange.

One day we sat down and thought, "Hey, we've got three healthy teenagers who complain that they have nothing to do." Guess what we decided to do? We put them to work! We realized that if we didn't delegate tasks around the house, we simply weren't going to be able to keep up with the pace of all the work that was required.

Through the process of delegation, I've learned that I can enjoy life more, in addition to getting more things done. I believe there are two basic reasons why you need to learn the art of delegating:

First, there is too much work for one person to do. Secondly, it is the best tool for empowering and growing people on your team.

Delegating work, however, is seldom easy. It involves the need to trust others, something that is not easy to do. It means that a portion of a person's rewards and setbacks depends on someone else's ability to perform. This leads to a fear of turning work over to someone else. But when people fear delegation, it dynamically restricts the amount of work that can ultimately get done, and it emphatically hinders the growth process in the lives of other individuals.

Recently, I read the story of young man's journey to a new understanding of life and the great need to delegate, simply by sitting down and chatting with a 72-year old gentleman on an airplane. As they chatted, the older man revealed that he was still a successful businessman. The younger man asked what made him successful and the older man obliged him. Then, near the end of the flight, the older man said, "The older I get, the quicker time seems to fly by. Enjoy life while you're young, son."

Later, the young man wondered how many times he'd heard someone say something similar during his life—forty, fifty, perhaps well over a hundred times? But for some reason, this particular incident finally compelled him to look up "time" in the dictionary.

The definition jumped off the pages at him. It read: "Time is a non-spatial continuum in which events occur in an apparently irreversible succession from the past through the present to the future."

To the young man, this definition seemed so concrete, so final, so powerful, that he began to realize—once time is gone, it can never be retrieved. This definition gave him new insight into why time is so precious, an insight he had never known or considered before.

Over the course of the next several days, the young man continued to think a great deal about time, tasks, and how he spent his life. Suddenly he came to the realization that, for the most part, time is a paradox. On the one hand, it put structure, meaning, and purpose into people's lives. On the other hand, he realized that time also caused him a great deal of stress at certain times in his life. Time had often kept him from enjoying himself.

From this, he concluded, that although the paradox of time would always exist, he figured that what he did with his time would be the best determinate factor concerning the quality of his life. His challenge, he realized, was one of finding balance. So he made a commitment to himself and his loved ones to live his life by three simple, key principles:

First, he realized "I have all the time I need to accomplish and finish the really important things I need to get done in life."

Second, he thought, "By completing these really important things, I will leave behind a very constructive legacy. My life will have been a meaningful adventure."

Third, he noticed, "If I'm going to maximize my potential in life, I must commit myself to getting some things done through others."

A leader may possess all of the necessary ingredients to being a great leader, but if he does not learn the art of delegation, then he will never find himself coaching a dream team like the one at NASA. Delegation is the most powerful tool leaders have. When a leader learns the art of delegation, they increase their own personal productivity as well as the productivity of their department or organization. Leaders who can't or won't delegate create a bottleneck to productivity.

I believe there are a number of reasons why leaders have a hard time delegating work. See if you can find yourself in one of these categories.

THE TRAINING TRADE-OFF

Foremost, many managers and supervisors have so much work to do that they feel paralyzed to offer any substantial investment of time to train other people on the team to do another task. Initially, delegation and planning do take quite a bit of time. It takes the time to teach, explain, and delegate things to others. However, a leader has to keep in mind that delegation pays huge dividends in the end.

My father prepared thousands of tax returns for people. He became a tax guru and saved people millions of dollars. Unfortunately for him, he did not enjoy doing people's taxes, but he could not seem to say "no" to the hundreds of people that came back to him year after year.

My dad was overburdened. However, he had a thought, "If I could actually prepare the tax work, then I could train our on-staff attorney and Randy to input the tax information onto the tax forms. Then, I'll just thoroughly review the forms before I sign off on them."

One thing that impressed me about my father was his willingness to take time out of his enormously busy day to train our attorney and myself to fill out the tax forms based on his interviews with the client. Day after day, hour after hour he trained us until we understood it.

By the time we got started, piles of our client's tax folders urgently needed completion. After a few weeks, we were able to catch up with the workload, complete the job on time and efficiently, and relieve my father of a world of stress. Had he not taken the time, as our leader, to delegate the work and train us, he would have filed hundreds of extensions and ultimately would have disappointed some people.

SOLVING DELEGATION CHALLENGES

Some leaders have a perfectionist tendency. These perfectionists have a great fear that if they delegate to someone else, it's just not going to get done right, or it won't get done in a manner that they believe it should be done. These leaders will analyze minutia to achieve perfection. Perfectionism can paralyze a team. It forces people to spend their time on low-input tasks rather than on high-output tasks. Sometimes this condition is referred to as the "paralysis of analysis."

How many times have you been afraid to delegate for fear that it won't be done exactly the way you'd do it?

At a recent seminar, several people were talking about the concept of delegation. They were huddled into a group, and each one began the conversation of how they desperately needed to delegate things. Each complained of how much they had to do, that they did not have enough time to do it and of how few resources they had to work with to get it all done.

One gentleman raised his hand in the air and said, "When we have discussions or disagreements like this, we have a brainstorming meeting. One of us writes the four 'M's on the board--manpower, method, machines, and materials. We know these are the only four categories of resources in the world. We know if we brainstorm long enough around these four M's, we're bound to find a solution to becoming more productive."

One of the participants spoke up and said, "I'm the founder of a not-for-profit organization, and mostly all we have are volunteers. We don't have the monies needed to include more manpower, machines, or materials, and as far as methods go, we're already as streamlined and efficient as we can be. My problem is, when I do give something for the volunteers to do, they don't do it as efficiently as I would like."

A young Texan spoke up and made a suggestion. He said, "I used to never delegate anything until I talked with a friend of mine who is a self-made millionaire. He's a man I respect and admire a great deal. He told me that success in life is like a cattle drive. Each steer represents a project or a task. There are a lot of these tasks, and they head in all different directions. The most important thing is not that they are heading straight ahead all the time, the most important thing is that they're just heading in the general direction of west."

The group had a good laugh, and they all learned a good lesson about delegation. Successful leaders cannot demand perfection from every steer in the herd. The successful leader keeps pushing things forward, realizing that some projects will need little attention and some more than others. The main thing is that things are heading in the right general direction.

As Ken Allen states in *The Effective Executive*, "Rarely is delegation failure the subordinate's fault. Maybe you picked the wrong person for the job, didn't train, develop or motivate sufficiently."

If you've had trouble with delegation in the past, don't give up. Try to determine why the problem occurred, learn from it, and try delegation again.

Many leaders also feel that delegating is in some form a sign of weakness. These people either internally feel or simply perceive that other people will think that they're passing work off to others is a sign of ineptitude, lack of strength, the inability to organize, or the inability to see things through to their ultimate conclusion.

Perhaps a hundred years ago being completely self-sufficient was a sign of strength, but in today's high information and fast-paced age, ignoring the opportunity to delegate means ignoring an incredibly valuable tool. It also means that you're working harder instead of smarter. Smart leaders learn how to get things done through others. It saves you time so that you can spend more time on the vital matters.

Some leaders don't delegate because they've become creatures of habit. They simply get so caught up in the fast pace of what they're doing that they never stop to ask the all-important question, "Could I get someone else to do this?"

Remember the adage: "When I let go, you grow." By letting go of certain tasks, you are actually helping people grow. There may be training involved, but that's a good thing. Someone grows from it. It may cost money, but time is a finite resource and money can always be made. Once time is gone, it is gone forever. Money invested in your team produces a great pay-off in the end.

Another reason why many leaders won't delegate is that they think their team is already overloaded. A few years ago, I was surprised to read a survey done by the American Management Association. In research among several large companies throughout the country, the AMA found that 50% of the people said that they could do more work.

It would be my recommendation to ask your team members if they could fit in some additional tasks. As you do, mention to them how important the task is, how important it is to the end result, and how much the team has to rely upon the task to accomplish its purpose. In other words, sell the task to the individual; don't just give people more work to do.

They need to know that you are relying on them and that you trust them to do a great job. Let them know why you've chosen them to do the task. This will provide them a great deal of meaning and purpose behind the task.

Another hindrance that keeps leaders from delegating is self-gratification. Some leaders enjoy doing the work themselves. They like the routines of busy work. They enjoy doing the nitty-gritty, day-to-day, bump-and-grind tasks. But when your head is down in the paperwork all of the time, you don't take the time to look up to administer your team.

The fact is, leaders need to free themselves of the many activities that don't necessarily go along with leadership. *Make a list of those activities that aren't indigenous to your role as a leader and plan on giving them away.*

LET GO AND REACH FURTHER

One Saturday afternoon, I was exhausted. I decided I'd stop by a local Chinese restaurant to sit down, relax, have a nice, warm meal and reflect on the week. As I sat there thinking about our church, I began to experience some mixed feelings. On the one hand, I was excited and thankful as to how God had blessed our church and how quickly it had grown. On the other hand, I was also quite concerned as to how we were going to meet the demands.

Being a little disconcerted, I grabbed my napkin and started to write. I began listing all of the things that needed to be done: visiting the new families of the church, overseeing the accounting of funds, cleaning the building, ordering food and preparing the church for Wednesday night Bible study, developing a training course for new Christians, developing a church membership course, counseling people who were having some problems, visiting those who were sick, and so on. The list completely filled my napkin.

As I finished my list and reflected on what needed to be done, I felt my chest pulling tight from the stress. *How was I going to pull this off?* Then it dawned on me. As I looked over the list, I noticed that there were some things that I didn't need to be involved in as a leader. I could give those tasks away to someone else. I also realized that there were things on that list that I couldn't give away, they are a part of my leadership role in the church, and no one else could fill that role. I also discovered that the best use of my time, as well as the best use of the enormous talent within our church, was to delegate tasks to competent people.

When I did eventually get around to handing these tasks out to people, believe it or not, they were actually thrilled with the opportunity to serve our church.

If you're the type of leader who is gratified with a heavy workload of activities, think of freeing yourself up from the clutter of tasks that can be done by someone else. Do what I did. Make a list of all of the activities that you're doing now. As you review your list, place a checkmark beside any activity that someone else could do. Maybe there's going to have to be a little bit of training involved to give that task away, but think of how much time it will free you up to do the most important things in your weekly routine down the road.

DELEGATION IS NOT DUMPING

Developing a proper atmosphere for delegating is crucial too. It's important to have a win-win environment. That's where everyone has respect for the leader, is heavily involved in a busy workload, and is having fun at the same time. Like bees around a hive, they have a sense of vision, mission, passion, and accomplishment. This type of nurturing environment is invigorating.

There are, however, other types of environments. There's the lose-lose environment, where people take tasks grudgingly. They don't have much respect for the leader, and they feel that they have been dumped on.

I remember one seminar where I had selected an individual for some role-playing. I was pretending to be her boss, and my job was to invite her to take on some additional tasks. As I talked with her about some new tasks, I noticed that she crossed her arms and gave me a stern look. Not really knowing why she seemed so agitated, I continued. I tried every conceivable tactic to hand over some additional work, but she wasn't buying into it. She didn't want to have anything to do with any additional work or me. It got everybody's attention, including mine. Finally, I asked her why she was so adamant about refusing to take some additional growth-grooming activities. When she responded, we were all a bit surprised!

She asked me the question, "You're my manager, right?"

I nodded and said, "Yes. That's right. Is there a problem with that?"

She responded, "Yes there is! The problem with my manager is that I don't trust her."

Wow! Did that bring a response from the seminar attendees! We all then engaged in the discussion of how important it is to have the leader positively connected with each team member, having his or her respect and admiration as a leader, as well as creating the right win-win environment conducive to delegating.

Another type of environment is the "win-lose" environment. This type of environment is the type of atmosphere where the people in power are perceived to be "dumping" workloads, not delegating.

There are some things you can do to keep the workplace environment more conducive to delegating. If you're struggling to have the kind of work environment that's right for delegating, consider taking your team through the following three phases:

1) The Discovery Phase: This is where you find out what kind of an environment you have. It also means discovering what kind of environment your team would like to have. What kind of environment is motivating, conducive to high-energy output, and delegating?

Suggestions: Have a team meeting. Ask the team to describe your environment in three words or less. Then, discuss everyone's choice of words. Call a brainstorming session to discuss ways you and your team can create a positive team environment that would be conducive to everyone working with subdued urgency, teamwork, and the ability to effectively delegate tasks to one another.

2) The Development Phase: This is where you begin implementing the results of your team meetings. Your task is to create an environment that is fun and upbeat. During the past several years, research has been done on the beneficial role of humor and laughter in the workplace. Many researchers have emphasized that humor and fun activities set within the work environment enhances productivity, creativity, and enthusiasm among employees. In fact, some researchers have stated that workers who make work upbeat and fun are almost twice as productive as workers who don't.

Suggestions: Give mini-workshops on laughter, play, and humor. Keep a camera ready to capture certain moments. Put funny posters up around the office. Do a once-a-week lunch get together and have fun. Incorporate fun in your meetings. Have magicians, humorists, or dramatists at a lunch-and-learn meeting.

3) The Delivery Phase: This phase emphasizes the actual delivery of the task. This phase is about how you deliver the task to the one you want to perform the task. Keep this thought in mind during this phase - poor delegators do a lot of telling, but successful leaders do a lot of selling. Delegation involves good salesmanship and persuasion, particularly on the front end of the task. If you don't sell it, they may not buy it.

After all, if they perceive it's just more work for the same pay, they probably won't be interested. But if you can show them why they need the task and what's in it for them, they'll be honored to take it.

Suggestions: Take time to explain the importance of the task and how you and the team benefit from it. Share your vision for the task and why you selected them as the right person for the job. Be specific. Explain to some small degree how you'd like the job accomplished, but reassure them that you're offering them to use their ingenuity to do it better and more efficiently in time. Explain also what is expected of them. Then, be willing to reward them for a job well done.

Mark Twain once said, "Never learn to do anything. If you don't learn, you will always find someone else to do it for you." Although he wasn't serious, there is a kernel of truth in his statement. The truth is you must always be looking for people to whom you can give tasks. The times that people will track you down to ask you for something to do will be rare. A leader must always be looking at ways of getting more done by using the strengths of others.

Let's take a survey and see what kind of leader you are when it comes to delegating. Remember to answer honestly.

WHAT KIND OF LEADER ARE YOU?

1. You gave a new worker a high profile assignment. He or she messed it up, big time. What do you do?

    A. Move the employee off the assignment and finish it yourself Make a personal note: This employee does not have the skills to handle big projects.

    B. No big deal, this stuff happens all the time.

    C. Go through the project with the employee and find out where he or she slipped up. Give him or her another assignment as soon as possible to test what he or she has learned.

2. A worker presents a completed job to you. What do you do?

    A. Go over it step by step, and point out areas where you would have done things differently.

    B. Briefly scan it and approve of the employee's efforts.

C. Spend a few minutes together and talk about the successes and failures he or she worked through.

3. An employee pops into your office with a decent plan to increase business, but it needs some work. What do you do?

 A. Your department is busy - put it on the back burner for now.

 B. Rework the idea yourself and implement it.

 C. Tell the employee to work on a more complete plan and report back to you in a week for more direction.

4. During an evaluation, you note an employee's habitual tardiness. After a week of being punctual, the employee comes in two hours late every day. What do you do?

 A. Tell him or her to show up on time. Communicate the importance of this every single day until he or she gets the message.

 B. You warned him or her once, and that should be enough.

 C. Hold another one-on-one meeting. Talk about any problems that may be causing the lateness. Suggest that he or she work later to make up for the lost time.

5. You end up being the last one in the office at night. Why is that?

 A. Somebody has to do the work around here, and you're ultimately responsible.

 B. You had a long lunch and your entire schedule got pushed back.

 C. You realize you could've delegated some of what you're working on; it won't happen again.

6. You see an employee having a difficult time with a customer. What do you do?

 A. Step in and take over. The employee can learn from watching you operate.

B. Observe from a distance and let the employee deal with it.

C. Stand and watch for a minute. If the employee starts to handle the situation, let him or her continue. If not, take over. Later, you go over what happened and how it could have been handled differently.

7. How do you approach a written evaluation for an employee?

A. Focus on the need for improvement. Discuss (or at least mention) every mistake and shortcoming, so the employee knows you're aware of them and that you're watching for progress from this point on.

B. You only need a half hour to finish it- evaluations don't carry that much weight with you.

C. Focus on one or two weak areas to improve. Be sure to mention an area where the employee excels or has improved noticeably.

If you answered mostly A, you're probably a micromanager. You prefer to work alone, and you're secure in your abilities, but you can't trust your employees to do the same good job. Your challenge is to increase employee competence through training and encouragement. Your assignment is to back off and see what happens.

If you answered mostly B, you might be the "invisible boss." For you, managing means just getting by. You show up for work every day, but emotionally you left the organization a long time ago. You've probably been in this job too long and have lost your enthusiasm. You fear making decisions, so you just let things go. Your assignment is to start talking with your employees and to get your motivation as a leader back into your heart.

If you answered mostly C, you are the "mentor boss." You have learned that your job is to help others get the job done. You can usually strike a balance between keeping your boss happy and keeping your workers satisfied and productive. You communicate well with your workers. You guide your employees without taking over the job - or stealing their initiative. You prepare them for better positions and greater responsibilities. Your assignment is to keep up the good work!

DELEGATION STEPS

1) The first step is the **decision**. This means you need to make a choice about "What is it that needs to be delegated?" or "What is it that should be delegated?" I would recommend that you do exactly what I did at the Chinese restaurant. Take a long lunch break and consider all the tasks that you're involved in as a leader. Make a list of all those activities. Then go through them one-by-one and separate those tasks that are indigenous to being a leader and those that aren't. Try to be aggressive about it. Which tasks can you give away? Don't even think about who you've got to do the job. Right now, all you want to do is to develop a list of those things that you don't need to be doing.

As you come up with those activities, I want you to write them down on the left-hand column of a piece of paper. Be sure to provide enough space between those activities so that you can write down the talents necessary for those activities.

Once you've developed a list of activities that you'd like to delegate, make another list. This time, list the people on your team. This is the second question you'll be asking, "Who is the right person for the job?"

Be sure to write the names of every team member you have. Write their names across the top of the paper. Again, as you write their names down on a piece of paper be sure to provide adequate space to write down their talents - their strengths and weaknesses.

As you consider the person's talent, you might also consider some other things about the person. First, consider their personality. Before you do this exercise, you might want to jump ahead to the chapter "Understanding Your Team." In this chapter, I talk about the four basic types of personalities you'll find on your team. One of the things that I've learned in leading people is the need to understand your team. Once you've discovered their personality traits and the characteristics, you'll be miles ahead in figuring out who is the right person for the job.

2) A second step is to **define his or her development stage.** A new hire would naturally be in the embryonic stage.. This is where they are relatively new at what's going on. They are adjusting, and learning more and more every day about how to do their job more effectively. They haven't mastered their job yet, nor have they developed a close relationship with you and the team yet. They are trying to understand your leadership style, and you feel the need to continually encourage them, provide training for them, share with them, and befriend them.

3) The next stage is the **development stage**. This describes a person on your team who has mastered their job and demonstrated proficiency. They've developed a relationship with you and the team, and have a basic understanding of what's going on around them. They even know and understand how to do some of the other tasks. They're firmly grounded, and you are beginning to see some potential mentoring qualities about them. They're developing the ability to train someone to do their job.

4) The next stage is the **leadership stage**. These people have not only mastered their job and have mastered several others. They understand the team vision and mission and are committed to seeing it accomplished. They are behind you as a leader, and they have the proven qualities of being a good team player. They've been involved in mentoring others on the team and training them how to do their job more efficiently. They are potential leaders. You can count on these people to do a good job. When you give these people a task, they inherently know what's required and do it.

There are other characteristics you might want to consider as well, but I believe these four characteristics that I have already mentioned should be a part of your consideration.

Now that you have the list of tasks that you'd like to delegate as well as the list of people who make up your team, I want you to focus on the list of activities you've written down. List the qualities required to perform each task. Make sure the qualities that you list that are needed for the task are also the qualities you list for the people to whom you will delegate. The chart below is an example of how you might want to work out the delegation process.

Find Who's Best For The Job (Sample)

MY TEAM	Activity To Delegate	Personality Type Required	Stage Of Development
John	Quality Control	Choleric	Leadership Stage
Mary	Data Processing	Melancholy	Development Stage
Sue	Training	Sanguine	Embryonic Stage
Steve	Customer Service	Melancholy	Embryonic Stage
George	Accounting	Sanguine	Development Stage

5) The next step, however, is the toughest. This is the step when you'll have to **sell the task to the team member**. Remember: poor delegators tell, successful leaders sell. People don't want to be managed; they want to be lead. They don't want to be dumped on, controlled, or handled. People want respect, admiration, honesty, and a sense of pride. They want everything you want as a leader. This is the step where you'll have to use tact and the ability to persuade. But, don't worry, I'll help you with it.

THE GOLDEN RULE OF DELEGATION

First, never delegate anything to anybody that you wouldn't be willing to do yourself, including making the coffee. This is the Golden Rule of Delegation. People can sense from you if this is a task you won't do yourself. You can't sell anything unless you're willing to buy into it yourself.

According to Mark Towers, in his book *Dynamic Delegation*, he warns leaders of delegating the following:

- Never delegate the task of selecting the right players.

- Don't delegate the task of motivating team members.

- Don't delegate evaluating fellow team members.

- Don't delegate the opportunity to reward the team.

- Don't delegate rituals.

- Don't delegate personal matters.

- Don't delegate items that help set precedent or create future policy.

- Never delegate long-range planning.

Towers also provides a list of what a leader might consider delegating:

- Delegate routines.

- Delegate tasks and projects that are the most unfamiliar to you.

- Delegate functions of your job that you enjoy least.

- Delegate some enjoyable things to others.

- Delegate tasks or challenges that will interrupt the routine of those in boring jobs.

- Delegate time to people so that they can cross-train one another.

- Delegate areas of your job that require technical expertise.

Secondly, discover what motivates each individual. Some people are motivated by money, by job security, personal growth, advancement, helping others feel good, and others by doing things they're good at. There are different strokes for different folks. Your job as a leader is to find out what it is that motivates the person. Part of selling is knowing who you're talking to.

In an article entitled *The Manager's Desk Reference* written by Charles and Cynthia Fink, they agree that ninety-nine percent of employees are motivated by one of the following seven needs:

- **Achievement**. These employees want the satisfaction of accomplishing projects successfully. They want to exercise their talents to attain success. They are self-motivated if the job is challenging enough, so provide them with the right work assignments and they will consistently produce.

- **Power**. These employees get satisfaction from influencing and controlling others. They like to lead and persuade and are motivated by positions of power and leadership. Give them the opportunity to make decisions and direct projects.

- **Affiliation**. These employees derive satisfaction from interacting with others. They enjoy people and find the social aspects of the workplace rewarding. Motivate them by giving them opportunities to interact with others: teamwork projects, group meetings, etc.

- **Autonomy**. These employees want freedom and independence. Allow them to make their own choices, set their own schedules, and work independently of others.

- **Esteem**. These employees need recognition and praise. Give them ample feedback and public recognition whenever possible.

- **Safety and security**. These employees crave job security, a steady income, health insurance, and a hazard-free work environment. Give these people predictable work with little risk or uncertainty. Also, salary and fringe benefits are very important to them.

- **Equity**. These employees want to be treated fairly. They probably compare work hours, job duties, salary, and privileges to those of other employees and will become discouraged if they perceive inequities.

Here's a suggestion. You might have a team meeting where you have a list of personal motivation factors. Write the following on a piece of paper:

- Job Security

- Personal Growth

- Fun

- Advancement

- Flex-time

- Rewards & Recognition

- More Money

- Team-Building Events

- Helping Others

- Free Food

- Other Ideas

Ask your team members to place a value on which ones mean the most to them. This will help provide you an insight into what personally motivates them.

As part of your "sales pitch," you'll now have an understanding of how you can sell the task. You see, everyone is tuned to the same radio station—WIIFM—the "What's In It For Me" radio station. When you discover what motivates them, you can spend some time discovering ways that the new task will appeal to that motivation factor. Once you've figured that out, you're on the right track to helping them to feel "buy-in" into the new activity.

Thirdly, the next thing you'll want to do is explain to them why you've chosen them for that particular job. You've chosen them because they had particular strengths in this area. This gives you a good time to encourage them about the positive qualities of their personality and work skills. Perhaps you'll want to give them past examples of how you've seen the type of strengths they possess.

The next step in the delegation process is expectations and boundaries. People need to know what's expected of them as well as the boundaries to which you will let them go. Explaining and defining limits is vital to the process of delegation.

In his book, *Dynamic Delegation*, Mark Towers notes that there are basically six levels of boundaries when it comes to delegating.

Boundary 1: The delegator says to the delegatee: "Examine the situation thoroughly. Bring me all the data you possibly can. I'll make the final decision."

As you can see, there is not a whole lot of delegating going on. The delegatee is simply involved in some investigative work without the powers of making decision. This decision is best implemented when you have someone who is new or unfamiliar with that particular area of concern.

Boundary 2: The delegator says to the delegatee: "Find the problem. Make a list of the possible plans of action we can take. Examine the pros and cons of each option. Then recommend a course of action, and I'll make the final decision."

Although the delegator is retaining the power to make important decisions, this boundary is best used with someone who has demonstrated a knowledge in a certain area, and you value their input. At this point, it gives the delegator a chance to explore the style of the delegatee.

Boundary 3: The delegator says to the delegatee: "Investigate the task thoroughly. Make a decision about the best course of action to take. Discuss the task and decision with me, but don't do anything until we've agreed upon our course of action."

At this point, the delegator has developed a trust and confidence in the abilities of the delegatee. Although the delegator values the judgment of the delegatee, the delegator is still gathering data about the delegatee and their ability to make independent decisions. In time, the desire of the delegator is to release decision-making to this delegatee.

Boundary 4: The delegator says to the delegatee: "I want you to handle this project. But   before you make any decisions and take any action, I want to give you some input. I want you to handle this your way, but let's talk first."

At this level, the delegator has developed a high level of trust in the delegatee's ability to handle the situation effectively and efficiently. Although there is still a check-and-balance attitude with the delegator, he or she still prefers that the delegatee handle this project within their abilities as a potential leader.

Boundary 5: The delegator says to the delegatee: "Go forward with this project. Complete it. Then come and tell me how it turned out."

This boundary implies a high degree of friendship and bonding. It also reveals the act of empowerment. Also, by asking the delegatee to provide feedback, the delegator maintains an ability to "stay-in-the-loop" of what's going on.

Boundary 6: The delegator says to the delegatee: "Go ahead and handle the situation. There's no need for you to tell me what you did." In effect, the boundary has been erased. Achieving this level may take years of people working together and becoming familiar with one another's abilities, habits, and way of processing. As far as expectations go, be sure to explain your expectations as thoroughly as possible. Ask the delegatee to paraphrase what they heard you say the expectations to be. This will help to ensure that they are on the right track.

Since everybody learns at different levels, you might even want to show the delegatee an example of what's expected. This type of person may be a kinesthetic learner requiring the need that you both tell and show them what's expected. In fact, most of us are kinesthetic learners. We first learn by hearing about what's expected, but we're not necessarily sure until we actually see an example of what's expected.

The next step in delegation involves instructions. Offer instructions to the delegatee, but leave room for them to do it in their own style. Don't micro-manage people. You may have to in the beginning, but you'll need to learn to develop trust in their ability to learn and do things on their own. Micro-managing people at a sustained level will destroy what you eventually want to accomplish. You'll never be able to develop competent people within your team. As General George Patton once said, "Never tell people how to do things. Tell them what to do, and they will surprise you with their ingenuity."

As you offer instructions, follow this model used at General Electric: I tell you how, you tell me how. I show you how, you show me how. Together, let's both observe the results.

Another way you might approach it is to offer some instructions and then ask the person how they feel they will approach the task. This will give you an opportunity to see if they're on track or not.

The final step in delegation is "empowering." This is when you have developed a trust in their ability to understand what is expected of them, they understand what they must do, and they know their boundaries. You then empower them to do it in their own style. But remember, before you let them do it on their own, you'll need to do two things. As you empower them, do the following:

1. Support: Be sure to provide them with the necessary tools and resources needed for them to succeed. If you don't provide the means for them to succeed, they'll give the task back to you for fear of failing. They'll also be less likely to want to receive any more tasks from you. You must train your people and give them whatever resources they feel they need to succeed.

2. Recognition: Be sure to provide them with recognition of a job well done. If they're half way through a project and on schedule, share with the rest of the team of how well they are doing. Recognition, reward, and praise are critical elements to keeping people happy and encouraged in the task that you give them.

PROBLEMS TO WATCH FOR

As you delegate, you'll need to keep in mind that there are two very common problems related to delegation. The first is inadequate results. If you're not receiving the results you need, revisit the issues of expectations and boundaries. Perhaps what the person needs is some training or clearer instructions on how to do the job. Maybe all they need is more time to learn the job. Remember, you didn't do this job perfect the first time, either. Ask them what they think is expected of them and what they might need in order to bring up their level of performance in the activity. Give them room to fail.

The second inadequate result is reverse delegation. Reverse delegation is the process of allowing employees to put their problems and work on your back. To make sure you don't encounter reverse delegation, understand the causes of reverse delegation and how to correct the problem. There are three common causes.

- **Unclear instructions**: Make sure your instructions are thorough and clear. Provide additional training and instructions and avoid sending double messages.

- **Lack of confidence**: Be a coach. Be an encourager. Provide the support necessary to build confidence.

- **Lack of resources**: Make sure they have the money, tools, supplies, training, and whatever else is necessary for them to succeed.

To help you remember the steps a leader must take in the delegation process, remember the simple acrostic formula from the word DELEGATE:

D - Decision: Making a decision about what you will delegate.

E -Enlisting: Selecting and selling the right person for the job.

L - Learning: Providing them expectations and instructions.

E - Empowerment: Learning to let go and let others do the task.

G - Growth: Delegation is about growth. Are they growing?

A- Achievement: Making sure they are achieving the stated goals.

T -Teaching: Can they teach others to do the job?

E -Encouragement: Always encourage people. They will love you for it.

As you can see, delegating tasks can be a powerful tool in the hands of an effective, peak performance leader. To do it correctly, you'll need to master the art of communication. That's why I want to tackle this delicate and important issue in the next chapter.

Chapter 6
The Peak Performance Essential - Communication

Communication within a team is everything. Team members must communicate effectively with each other, and the leader must communicate effectively with the team. Without effective and efficient communication, all is lost.

Several years ago, I read a funny article that described the hazards of poor communication. It went like this:

A couple of older men rode the train out of London when it came to one of the stops along the way. One of the men asked the other, "Is this Wembley?"

"No," cried the other gentlemen, "This is Thursday!"

"Fine," said the first, "Let's get off and get a drink."

How often can we relate to that? Just because it was said doesn't mean it was understood. How many times have you said something so clearly to someone that no one could possibly misunderstand, but they did?

As a corporate trainer, I've witnessed firsthand how often employees have expressed the need for the quality and the quantity of effective communication in the work environment. I've heard the sad stories of management encouraging open communication, but only offering lip service instead of developing a way to make it happen. Others have contended that their organizations believe that posting notices on bulletin boards and sending out memos is adequate communication. Still others say they receive vague instructions that are difficult to follow.

Ineffective communication often results in disaster for an organization. It eventually degrades into poor cooperation and coordination between team members, lower productivity, an undercurrent of tension, gossip and rumors, and increased turnover and absenteeism.

COMMUNICATION IS MORE THAN WORDS

Experience shows that leaders can improve internal communications in many ways. The first thing you need to understand is that communication is a two-way street. Communication isn't over just because you finished delivering your message. Good, effective communication involves speaking, listening and body language. In fact, when it comes to speaking, a person needs to consider more than just the words. Body language includes our body positioning, our facial expressions, and the tone of our voice. Here are some examples of how to use body language to improve communication.

1) Research has shown that what we say (our words) has only an 8 percent impact on the listener. Our body language, however, accounts for 55 percent, while our voice counts for 37 percent. In other words, our body language combined with our voice intonation provides an incredible 92 percent of the message received. That means that "what we say" has less of an impression on someone else than "how we say it."

If you walk into your boss' office next Monday morning and you see him with a stern look on his face, his arms are tightly crossed, and he's feverishly tapping his foot, does that communicate anything to you?

Remember, the next time you want to communicate something, remember that your facial expressions, intonation, and body language are all going to say volumes before your words do.

2) The second thing that I suggest is to put more emphasis on face-to-face communications with your team. Don't rely on texts, emails, bulletin boards, memos, and other forms of written communication. Written communication does have its place, but to rely on it is dangerous. You assume too much when you rely on written communication.

Several years ago, I had the opportunity to do some one-on-one coaching with an individual in the financial field. He was sharp, well groomed, and articulate. As we chatted about business, he clearly gave me every indication that he was also well educated. As we did some reading together, I realized that he suffered from dyslexia. When it was his turn to read some passages in a book, he would struggle with certain words. At times, he would pull a different meaning from the passage than what was intended.

Later, I started to wonder, "How many other people suffer from dyslexia? How many are simply poor readers or struggle with reading comprehension?" I also asked myself, "How many people are uninformed simply because they are challenged with reading?"

While in Fort Lauderdale, Florida serving as an associate pastor of a church, I had the privilege of becoming closely acquainted with our pastor's brother in-law, who also was a member of our church and head of the church board. He was a sharp businessman and ran one of the most successful equipment rental stores in south Florida. Outside of the fact that he was a millionaire and succeeded at whatever he did, he was a gentleman who quietly disclosed to me that he couldn't read. He was raised in a poor family and forced to go to work at a young age; consequently, he never had the opportunity to learn how to read. I was amazed. Though this man had the outward appearance of a great education, he had never learned how to read. This man relied on excellent oral communication skills all of his life.

3) Communication involves effective listening skills. Once you learn how to listen to employees, your leadership skills will improve dramatically. You'll get better feedback, communicate better, and solve more problems.

Here are some pointers that will improve your listening skills, and help you get the most out of each meeting with an employee:

THE BAD LISTENER FITS THIS MOLD

- **Mind reader**. This person hears very little of what the other person is saying because they're busy asking the question, "What is this person really trying to say and why?"

- **Rehearser**. This person mentally tunes people out thinking, "Here's what I'll say next."

- **Fitter**. Some call this selective listening - hearing only what you want to hear.

- **Dreamer**. This is the person who drifts off during a face-to-face conversation only to end up asking the question, "What did you say?" or "Can you repeat that again, please?"

- **Identifier**. This person refers everything they hear to their own experience. Consequently, they are not really hearing what the person is truly saying.

- **Comparer**. This happens when you get sidetracked assessing the person that you're conversing with. You look them over and consider their appearance or something else about them attempting to get a "fix" on who they are.

- **Derailer**. This person changes the subject too quickly. It gives the other person the idea that you're not interested.

- **Sparer**. You hear what's said but quickly belittle it or discount it. That puts you in the same class as the derailer.

- **Placater**. This person agrees with everything they hear just to be nice or to avoid a conflict. This doesn't necessarily mean you're a good listener.

THE GOOD LISTENER DOES THIS

Here are some things you'll want to do when you do encounter a conversation with a team member:

- Stop what you're doing and clean off your desk when meeting with a team member. If there are loose papers on your desk, you'll unconsciously start to fiddle with them - and may even start to glance over them. Clear your desk for every conversation with an employee, so you can focus your attention on what they're saying.

- Take a conscious note of the color of the team member's eyes. Train yourself to notice eye color at the start of every conversation. It ensures that you will make significant eye contact - which leads to more productive conversations. However, it's important keep from focusing on their eye color so much that you're actually hindered from really listening to what is being said. Duh!

- Train yourself to ask questions instead of making statements. For example, "Sue, don't forget that the Anderson report needs to be in on Monday morning." Rather, say, "How is the Anderson report coming along, Sue? Any problems with meeting the deadline?" By asking questions you'll start a dialogue, and you never know what you might learn.

- Train yourself to ask questions that reflect and paraphrase what the team member has said to you. For example, ask, "John, are you saying that Ken and Mary are having difficulty with closing the sale? And, you feel that the reason is because the customer doesn't have all the information necessary to make a decision?" This allows for you to be absolutely sure of what is being said. I can't tell you how many times this little tactic has worked for my wife and I whenever we don't see eye-to-eye on something! It has cleared the air on a lot of things.

- Learn to "lubricate" conversations. Phrases such as, "Yes, I see" and "I understand" or even a simple nod of the head do two things: 1) They show that you're listening, and encourage the other person to keep talking; and 2) They keep your attention focused.

- Don't blurt out questions as soon as the employee is finished speaking. It looks as if you were formulating your reply rather than listening. Before you ask a question, use the paraphrase technique. For example: "So what you're saying is..." then ask your question, "Well, let me ask you this..." This cuts down on miscommunication.

- Don't smile the whole time. A lot of managers do this because they think it sends a friendly message. It can, but people also often mistake it for mental absence or a sign that you're not taking them seriously. Save smiles for humorous remarks.

- Another way to look at beefing up your listening skills is to follow the guidelines using the word "listen" in an acrostic:

L: Lean forward. This shows you are ready to listen.

I: In focus. This means eye contact. It means eliminating distractions.

S: Silence. Remain silent until they're done. You don't learn by talking.

T: Take notes. Take notes if you need to. Ask for permission first.

E: Empathize. Show empathy, not sympathy. Try to understand their view.

N: Nod. This shows that you're listening.

4) A fourth ingredient to communicating better at work is to practice the open door policy.

Don't just talk open door, practice it by walking around and talking to your team members. Allow people to disagree and to come up with new ideas. As Sam Walton, the founder of Wal Mart stores, once said, "The key to success is to get out into the store and listen to what the associates have to say. It's terribly important for everyone to get involved. Our best ideas come from clerks and stockboys."

I would recommend to set a time each day to listen from employees so they can come and share their concerns and ideas. Make sure you let the employees know what that time is. You also have work, and having a completely open door policy that allows all employee to come in to your office anytime, which keeps you from getting your work done.

When they do come in to express an idea or concern, they expect you to respond. Make sure you do. If you're going to get back with them later, do it. If you'll think about it and consider implementing their idea only to eventually find that their idea won't work out, give them the courtesy of knowing that you gave it considerable thought and tell them why you feel it won't work out. This allows them to know that their voice is heard and that you count on them to be communicative. When you follow up on such action, this shows them that you respect them and count on their involvement. Concentrate on building credibility with your team members. Leaders who lack credibility and fail to create a climate of trust and openness aren't believed - no matter how hard they try to communicate.

5) Another thing to consider when communicating with team members, fellow leaders, and customers, is to use the T.A.C.T. method:

T: Think before you speak. The first thing that pops into your head is not always what you should say. Learn to pause before you say anything. Consider the person you're talking to, and customize the best response for that person.

A: Apologize for saying the wrong thing. Tactful leaders apologize immediately when they have said the wrong thing. Be sure not to use excuses, and don't pass the buck to someone else. Own up to it if you're in the wrong. Remember, you lead by example.

C: **Converse** with people, don't compete. Don't try to compete with the people you talk to. Don't push your opinions on them. Don't bully them. And don't try to win arguments that don't even exist. Treat every conversation as an equal exchange of information, ideas, and opinions.

T: **Time** what you say. Successful communication means timing. Don't speak when you're angry, or distracted, or too busy to really talk. And don't speak to someone else who is too angry, distracted, or busy to talk either.

BUILDING COHESION

According to the Hay Group, in a study observing 75 components of employee satisfaction, they found that teams are happiest when the top leadership effectively communicates in three critical areas:

1. Helping employees understand the company's overall business strategy.

2. Helping employees understand how they contribute to achieving key business strategies.

3. Sharing information with employees on how the company is doing - and how the employee's own division is doing relative to the whole company.

The Kaufmann Foundation in Kansas City engaged me as a communications consultant for certain projects. When I arrived, the leadership gave me a tour of the facility and a brief run-through of each department. In fact, the tour was based on the flow of paperwork and the operations from one step to the next. The whole operation absolutely impressed me. I could see how one department was totally dependent upon the other. I actually got excited. It occurred to me after a couple of weeks that the leadership needed to provide this same tour for everyone within the organization. If I got excited after seeing the whole operation, what would happen to the team if they could see it? What kind of value could they see placed on each individual's role and the team cooperation needed in order to do an efficient and on-time job?

How valuable this could be in building motivation and value into each workstation! The Kauffman foundation, as organized as they were, could have benefited from implementing the three critical areas already discussed to create a more cohesive organization.

According to the *Management Intelligence Report* by Regan Communications in Chicago, the latest trend in corporate America is "knowledge management"— the ability to communicate and gather an organization's collective knowledge into one area, so that all employees can gain from it. It requires effective communication and many companies over the years have benefitted from it. The report found:

- IBM consultants have cut proposal-writing time from an average of 200 hours down to 30 hours because they now can easily share information with each other.
- Xerox Corporation has developed "Eureka," an expert database. The average repair time needed for a Xerox copier reduced by 50 percent because of the information found on Eureka.
- Technical support reps at Dell Computer report that they can now solve more problems with a single call, thanks to a communication management system that advises them on what questions to ask and how to fix certain problems.
- W.L. Gore and Associates uses Lotus Notes and an intranet to tap into customers' needs and relay them to a product development team. The development team can then quickly devise customized products to meet those needs. This process used to take weeks; now, it can be done in days, or sometimes even hours.

Effective communication is essential. However, we're going to take communication one step further. We're going to take a look at how people are wired for communication. Not everybody is wired the same. Of course – you knew that!

Let's tap into the wiring mechanism. To do so, we'll take a look in the next chapter at the four basic personality types you have on your team. Each of these personalities have their own way of giving and receiving communication. Learning these styles will make you a master communicator. Let's take a look!

Chapter 7
Building Team Chemistry
The Peak Performance Way

As Butch Cassidy once said to the Sundance Kid, "Who are those guys anyway?" At times, we want to ask the same question about our team members, our supervisors, as well as the people who live in our own home. Every day we come to the same conclusion, "Everybody's different!" In fact, we're usually convinced that most people are weird, except us. Though we might not actually say it, we're usually thinking: "What is it about people? Why can't they see things the way I do? After all, I'm normal and I think rationally? Why can't they?"

Though we'd like everybody to see things the way we do, everybody is different. That makes our world work. Diversity is a strength, not a weakness. Diverse backgrounds, cultures, languages, personalities, and age groups have the power to bring a perspective you couldn't get without it. As a leader, you need to appreciate diversity and learn how to tap into its power. Whether you like your team or not, you need to learn how to make the most of it. Figuring out how to harness the potential within the diversity of your team will help you build a masterpiece.

When Michelangelo was ready to carve the statue of David, he spent months selecting the right marble. He knew the quality of the raw material would determine the beauty of the finished product. He also knew he could change the shape of the stone, but he couldn't transform the basic ingredient. Every masterpiece he made was unique, for even if he had wanted to, he would not have been able to find a duplicate piece of marble. Even if he cut a block from the same quarry, it wouldn't have been exactly the same. Similar, yes, but not the same.

We were all born with our own kind of raw material, our own rock. Some of us are granite, some marble, some alabaster, and some sandstone. Our type of rock doesn't change, but our shapes can be altered. So it is with our personalities. We start with our own set of inborn traits. Some of our qualities are beautiful with strains of gold. Some are blemished with fault lines of gray. Our circumstances, IQ, nationality, economics, environment, and parental influence can all play a part in molding who we are. No matter how we're shaped and what shape we take on, our rock beneath us remains the same.

In this chapter, I'd like for you to discover your type of personality as well as the personalities that make up your team. Once you do, you will be forever transformed in understanding what people are made of, who they really are, why they act the way they do, how they process information, and how to help them amplify their strengths and overcome their weaknesses. This will be your ticket into creating a dynamic team chemistry.

THE FOUR BASIC PERSONALITY STYLES

About four hundred years before the time of Jesus, Hippocrates, the Greek physician later noted as "The Father of Medicine" offered a theory that revolutionized the medical world at the time. He believed certain human moods, emotions, and behaviors were caused by body fluids. He systematized this theory into four basic "temperaments" or personality types:

1) The Choleric (hot-tempered)

2) The Sanguine (cheerful)

3) The Melancholic (depressed)

4) The Phlegmatic (calm)

He believed that each person's body organs produced an excess of bile, phlegm, black bile, and blood (the four "humors").

His theory stated that whichever fluid substance was produced in excess within that person's body would then determine a person's basic personality type.

Over the years, medical evidence has proven that a person's body fluids doesn't have anything to do with what personality style a person has. However, Hippocrates stumbled onto something that has been well accepted and has been the rigid study of both the medical community and science as well. His concept that all people can be into four basic personality types has revolutionized our world. Further, psychologists in the early twentieth century have tried to expound on this subject and develop it into their own perspective. This has yielded a variety of branches of personality assessments, but they all stem from the four basic personalities that Hippocrates initially defined many years ago.

Eventually, in the 1950s, Isabel Myers and her mother, Katheryn Briggs, through their study of the works of famed Swiss psychiatrist and psychotherapist Carl Jung, expounded on Jung's work and developed what is now known as the *Myers-Briggs Type Indicator* (MBTI), a system widely used in business and education today. However, their work took the four basic personality types and took it a bit farther when they expanded it into 16 personality styles. You can take a deeper look at these at www.myersbriggs. org.

Throughout the past 50 years, a number of other psychologists got involved which has produced a variety of other models as well. Perhaps you've been subjected to one of them: such as the Personal Profile System (PPS) or DiSC model, the Wilson, the Tracom System, and the Tony Alessandra "Platinum Rule" model, to name a few. As different as each of these are, they all are designed to achieve the same goal – to determine who really you are. In spite of their variations, they support Hippocrates' initial findings that there are four basic types of personalities.

To keep it simple, let's just keep this chapter to the basic four. It will give you a great head start in discovering how you're wired, as well as the tendencies of those around you.

HOW YOUR PERSONALITY DEVELOPED

There is an entire field of study dedicated to understanding the genetic components of your personality. This field of study is called behavioral genetics. Through this field of study we've learned much of what you already knew. When you were conceived in your mother's womb you received DNA from both of your parents, which contains the genetic makeup of not only your parents, but your grandparents and great grandparents as well. How ever those codes are written in your specific DNA, you receive a combination of all four personality traits. In other words, you are a complete amalgamation of having all four personality styles: the Choleric, Sanguine, Melancholy, and Phlegmatic. What depicts our certain type of personality style is the one surfacing as the most dominant trait. That dominant trait becomes your basic personality style. Even though you are made up of all four personality styles, like genes, there are personalities that become more dominant than others.

While the science of behavioral genetics is much more involved than I've discussed, I think you can get a general idea of how you came to be you, in terms of personality. The reason I've written a chapter in this book about personalities is because even though many people have had their personality tested, they simply have no idea what to do with that knowledge. They don't realize how powerful that knowledge is. Plus, if you're a leader, it's an invaluable tool to understanding your team and developing them into peak performance players. But why?

A person's personality has an enormous impact on how they process words and information, how they act and react to given situations, how they relate to other people, what kind of mood they'll have based on circumstances and events, the kind of talents and natural skills they have, and even how they view you and the rest of the world. As a leader, when you grasp an understanding of these things, you will begin your journey into an understanding of people that seems almost magical.

Before we begin, let me inform you that your personality will begin with a raw natural appearance in your early years. But, personalities can change over time. While you'll always have your most dominant personality as the basis of who you are, there are other things in life that will impact your personality and hopefully mold it into something very powerful – such as culture, age, maturity, family lifestyle, race, nationality, and life experiences.

For example:

- A harsh, outspoken Choleric may learn to be more careful with their words over time as they learn how words can hurt a Sanguine and even de-motivate a team.

- A non-detailed Sanguine may eventually learn how important it is to take the painstaking time of gathering facts and putting together detailed charts so that the Melancholies are happy and can do their job more effectively.

- A perfectionist Melancholy may eventually learn that their endless need for more thorough information or the need to make sure all the "I's are dotted and the "T's" are crossed is keeping the company from reaching its deadlines for customers, and will thus need to curb back their perfectionist compulsion a bit.

- The relaxed Phlegmatic may realize that their natural tendency to be quiet in the conference room isn't helping the team in coming up with new ideas.

All in all, your dominant personality is what you've got to work with. Identifying it and understanding its strengths and weaknesses (as well as those on the team) will help you to become the best leader you can be.

Later in this chapter, you'll have the opportunity to test yourself to see just exactly which personality style is most dominant within you. You might also see a combination of two or three that come out on top. Determining your personality style allows you to more fully understand and accept your natural strengths and weaknesses. It allows you to understand who you are, why you feel the way you do, and why you think the way you think.

You might be asking the question, "Can I really take all the people in the world, put them into four little boxes called 'personality styles' and claim that I now understand them?" Of course not. People are far more complex than what a single personality type can describe. What these personality styles do for us is simply give us a shorthand tool for improving our understanding of why people act, think, and speak the way they do.

WHY UNDERSTANDING PERSONALITIES IS A BIG SECRET TO LEADERSHIP SUCCESS

When you begin to fully comprehend these four basic personality styles, the eyes of your understanding will be enlightened. It will open up a whole new world of understanding for you. Without this knowledge, you're clueless to some extent. But, with this knowledge there comes power – especially when you apply it!

When you grasp the knowledge of personalities, you have an insight that gives you the leading edge. It's almost like having the other team's playbook. When you can really understand yourself and how other people on your team are wired, you can:

- Find a communication approach that will be much more effective to that individual.

- Match people with the right job assignments they will most likely enjoy and perform successfully – a much-needed ability to build a peak performance team.

- Find the right kind of strategies for motivating individuals to peak performance.

- Understand what kind of information you'll need to enable a person to comprehend and to understand the expectations of the project and are motivated to do it.

- Find the right approach to build team unity and communication

- And the list goes on!

MY FUN CHALLENGE WITH A CHOLERIC

Several years ago, my two teammates and I were stranded in an airport late one evening after conducting four days of intense, all-day management training courses in four different cities throughout the Northeast part of the U.S. The weather was bad, it was nearing 10:00 p.m. and we were exhausted. Then, the airline cancelled our flight. We scrambled to find a plane to get us to the next city. For the most part, we kept our cool. Everything was fine until our teammate, Mary, decided to scold the two of us.

Chris and I were tired of cramming a week's worth of suits and starched shirts into a carry-on bag. So, we brought a larger suitcase and decided to check our baggage on the plane. Now that our next plane was delayed and we would have to take an unscheduled flight, we knew that we were going to be held up at the baggage claim counter once we got to the next city. Mary couldn't believe it. She couldn't get over the fact that Chris and I had brought luggage too big to carry on. She knew this was going to create a problem for us at baggage claim once we landed. Mary let us know with very direct words that she couldn't believe we couldn't put a week's work of clothes into our carry-ons. I'll have to admit, I was a little embarrassed that a woman (typically known for bringing too many clothes during travel) was giving us men a lesson on travel.

Chris and I assured her that we would be fine. But that wasn't good enough. She yelled out in frustration, "You guys have penalized the team! Now we're going to have to wait for baggage at the next airport and look how late it is!"

Tensions were somewhat alleviated once we found a plane heading to the city of our destination. We boarded the plane, and settled down exhausted into our seats. It was around midnight when we finally landed. We couldn't wait to get to our hotel room to get a brief night's rest. All we needed was a quick run by the baggage claim to retrieve our bags and we were off. Mary was still fuming over the fact that we had to make this extra jaunt to the baggage claim area before grabbing a cab and heading to the hotel.

Once we got to baggage claim, the bags were already circulating through the carousel. "Great!" we all thought, "We'll just grab our bags and go." Then I added, "See Mary, all of that worry for nothing." Mary didn't say a word.

Chris saw his luggage the moment he got there and yanked it off of the carousel. Now all I needed was mine. But where was it? We all stood there trying to act as patiently as we could, even Mary. When the carousel finally came to a halt and my baggage wasn't there, I knew I was in for it. Mary had had it with us. She proved her point and she wanted each one of us to know it. She came straight to me and said, "See Randy, I told you this might happen! You've now penalized the team. You've penalized the team! Way to go!"

Chris stood there in awe. He couldn't believe Mary had gotten into my face and was now scolding me. He began to fume.

Meanwhile, I sheepishly headed over to the baggage claim office to share my misfortune. While I was making a claim of lost baggage, Chris decided to let Mary have it. He couldn't believe she was so direct and forceful about her feelings. "How could you say that to him?" he asked. "You're so blunt!"

While I was overhearing their conversation, I was reminded of what I teach in management classes on personality types. Mary is a choleric. She sees things in black and white. She feels the need to express herself directly. It is a natural part of her personality. She didn't really mean anything negative by it. In fact, she was right. I did penalize the team. As I walked out of the baggage claim office, I went right to Mary and admitted my mistake. I apologized, told her I had learned my lesson and it was now time to get to the hotel for some much-needed rest. That was all Mary needed to hear.

From that moment on, she was fine. In fact, on our way to the hotel she and I laughed about the incident. All of this befuddled Chris. He was still upset. He couldn't believe that I was letting her get away with all of this. All the way to the hotel, Chris fumed, and didn't say one word in the car.

The moment we got to the hotel and Mary had checked in, Chris stopped me. "How could you let her get away with that, Randy?" he asked. "She blasted you in the face with a verbal attack, but you've said nothing about it to her. Why?"

On the way to our room, I shared with Chris about Mary's personality. I told him why she said things the way she did. Although he wasn't fully convinced that I should let her off the hook, he somewhat understood.

Later the next day, we all discussed the incident and our own personality traits. Chris brought up the subject of Mary's direct verbal approach. Mary assured him that she meant nothing by it, she was only stating the facts as she saw them. Eventually, we all had a good laugh about it, and Chris learned something about how understanding people's personality styles can help you get along better with others.

By understanding the four different types of personality styles, you'll begin to see how this information can transform you and the entire team. In this chapter, you'll be able to see how it's possible for someone to be mismatched in a particular job situation, and how certain behavior, good or bad, can often follow our style. You'll also see that there is no such thing as a "good" or "bad" style. You'll discover in each style there are various strengths and weaknesses.

As you gain an understanding of the personality styles, you can see them reflected in your colleagues, giving you insight about their work habit and values. By understanding their contributions, strengths, and weaknesses, you can work more effectively with them. You'll be able to communicate better with people and understand what it is that makes them tick.

Let me offer you two pieces of advice. The first is from Tony Alessandra. In his audio program, *Mastering Your Message*, he mentions the need to follow the Platinum Rule: "Do unto others as they'd like done unto them." His assertion is that when you deal with people who possess different styles, you should alter your own behavior to fit their style if you want to achieve maximum results. What Tony means is simply this: the behavior adjustments will typically be talking faster or more slowly; altering your level of emotional display; or perhaps even focusing on the meaning behind what the other person says, based on their personality style. While this might seem a little insincere, knowing how to reach people in the course of their own natural style makes them feel more comfortable, more validated, and more willing to open lines of communication.

The second piece of advice is to combine Tony's Platinum Rule with Socrates' immortal words, "Know thyself." Through an understanding of yourself, as well as others, you'll be able to build a bridge of relationships and knowledge that you've never known before.

WHAT'S YOUR TYPE?

First, let's begin with a survey. While this survey might produce some useful information about yourself and your team members, it doesn't purport to tell you everything. Try it out on yourself first. Later, you'll want to consider taking your entire team through this survey to see what kind of personalities you might have on your team.

I want to give you a fair warning before you begin this survey. It's important to remember that as you take this survey you must be honest with yourself. Sometimes people tend to want to be someone they're not, or they think a certain attribute characterizes them when it really doesn't. The best way to find out if you're being honest with yourself is to discuss these answers with someone who knows you well.

Here's how to begin. In the survey below, choose the one statement that best describes you when you're working with your team. Both statements may be true of you, but choose the one that applies to you in the most situations, most often, and with the most people. Then, circle the letter in front of that statement.

PERSONALITY SURVEY

1. (D) I am often direct and frank in team meetings.
   (C) I tend to be reserved and careful in team meetings.

2. (D) I take control when there are crisis situations.
   (C) I tend to be more reflective in a crisis to see what happens before taking action.

3. (B) My decisions within the team are based on gut feelings that I have or issues that are raised by members within the team.
   (A) My decisions are usually based on facts, logic, and specific information that I have or are communicated by team members.

4. (A) I tend not to express my emotions and feelings to team members.
   (B) I often feel the need to express my emotions and feelings to team members.

5. (D) I usually have something to contribute during team meetings or conversations.
   (C) I seldom say anything in team meetings or discussions.

6. (C) I am careful and contemplative about taking risks and accepting new and difficult challenges.
   (D) I am quick to take risks and accept new and difficult challenges.

7. (B) My facial expressions and enthusiasm in conveying my views or responding to the views of others are typically greater than most people I know.
   (A) I tend to show little emotion in conveying my views or reacting to the views of others.

8.   (A)   I am usually a bit difficult to get to know in interpersonal situations and business situations.

      (B)   I feel like I am easy to get to know in both situations.

9.   (C)   I usually make decisions more slowly and with much forethought when I know my team will be affected.

      (D)   I usually can make decisions quickly, spontaneously, and in the "heat of the moment."

10.   (B)   I am able to adapt to changes in the schedule and to the ideas of the people around me.

      (A)   I am more rigid and disciplined about how I spend my time.

11.   (D)   I tend to use strong language and straight-to-the-point views when communicating to my team members. I am comfortable in stating my opinions.

      (C)   I tend not to raise my voice, use a harsh tone or express my views, feelings, and opinions to team members.

12.   (C)   I emphasize planning and detailed information about who should do what, how it should be done and when.

      (D)   My conversations with team members usually focus on personal experiences and other people in my life.

13.   (A)   My conversations with team members are almost alwaysfocused on my job, professional experiences and the work of other people.

      (D)   My conversations with team members are mostly about them, their families, and making sure that I am liked by everyone on the team.

14.   (D)   I tend to sometimes bend the rules to fit my needs and the team's needs.

      (C)   I always follow policies and rules in getting things done, and I encourage team members to do the same.

15.   (B)   My body language and facial expressions tell people right away, and with little doubt, what I am thinking and feeling.

      (A)   My body language and facial expressions tend to be more reserved so as to disguise my true feelings and personal thoughts about team members.

16.   (B)   I like to be out among my team members to get things done and to elicit their ideas.

      (A)   I prefer to work alone and not be encumbered by the thoughts, ideas and feelings of other team members.

17.   (D)   I enjoy introducing myself to new team members and am willing to talk to them about myself and personal matters.

      (C)   I usually let new team members introduce themselves to me rather than approaching them first, and I am reluctant to get too personally involved.

18.   (D)   In expressing myself and my views to the team, I often use statements such as "I think... " "I feel. .." and "I believe that . .. "

      (C)   In expressing myself and my views to the team, I often use statements that defend and justify my beliefs, such as "According to others I have spoken to. . ." or "Based on..." or "Others have found that..."

Now, count how many times you have circled each letter: and put the number in the space below corresponding with the appropriate letter:

A_____ B_____ C_____ D_____

Which letter has the highest number?

More "A's" means you're probably a "Choleric."

More "B's" means you're probably a "Sanguine."

More "C's" means you're probably a "Melancholy."

More "D's" means you're probably a "Phlegmatic."

Now that you've finished the survey, have you determined what personality style you have? Do you think it's accurate? If not, ask someone who knows you well to go over it with you. If you think you've got an accurate rate of your personality style, read the rest of the chapter to find out more about yourself as well as the other people on your team.

While there are many books out there concerning personality styles, one of my favorite is a book by Florence Littauer. In her book, *Personality Plus*, Littauer does an excellent job thoroughly discussing and explaining the differences of each one of these personalities. For years and in countless cities, I have encouraged thousands of leaders to purchase Florence's book. I carry it with me during my travels, and I believe it is required reading for all people, not just leaders. I've had many managers who've told me by way of email that their careers have taken on a more positive and dynamic change from my course on personality styles. I owe a lot of my knowledge to people like Florence Littauer, Tim LaHaye, and others who've written elaborately and in simple terms about this subject.

I recently had a manager who sent me an email sharing how transformed he was after one of my seminars. He was so excited from what he had learned from my 3-hour session on personalities that I felt compelled to encourage him to purchase Littauer's book. He did. After reading her book, he wrote me back thanking me for the recommendation and shared with me how powerfully it had impacted him. He was so changed by it that he decided to purchase the book as a Christmas gift for everyone in his family. That's not a bad idea! Whether it's Littauer's book, or mine, plan to give out as many of these books as you can. Sowing the seeds that bless and benefit other people is the greatest form of leadership I know!

A QUICK DIAGNOSIS

I can generally determine a person's personality in less than ten seconds. Having studied and taught this information for over 15 years, I can size a person up very quickly with just a few questions or statements. In fact, let me give you a quick general step you might want to use to determine the kind of personality you're dealing with, especially when it comes to selecting someone you're not for familiar with but needs to be assigned a specific task.

One of the quickest ways I've found determine a person's personality is to begin with what I call the "Extrovert / Introvert question." I usually ask them very politely, "How do you see yourself, as an extrovert type of person or more of an introvert type of person?" If they're not sure, ask them, "Do you like to talk in a group and feel the need to be very involved in a meeting so that you're voice is heard, or are do you tend to stay quiet and more reserved giving other people the liberty to talk?"

Right away, about ninety percent of the people you'll speak with will tell you which category they fall in. You'll have to ask the other ten percent more questions.

The extroverts or ones who like to have their voice heard in a meeting are the Cholerics and the Sanguines. The introverts or ones who would prefer to stay quiet are the Melancholy and the Phlegmatics. Once you've narrowed it down to these two groups, you can proceed to dig a little deeper.

For the extroverts, I'll usually begin with the question, "In a business meeting, do you enjoy small talk or do you like to just get down to the facts?" If a person is into small talk, they are a Sanguine. If they like to avoid small talk and get down to business, they are a Choleric.

For the introverts, I'll usually begin with the question, "When it comes to working on a project, how important is having all the facts before you begin?" If they tell you they couldn't begin

the project without having all the facts, they are most likely a
Melancholy. If they hesitate at all on that question, and or mention
to you that facts are important but they could begin on the project
without having all the facts, they are probably a Phlegmatic.

THE DRIVEN CHOLERIC

Cholerics possess the abilities to potentially be the greatest
leaders of all. They are driven, challenge oriented, and forward-
looking people. They love to start businesses, lead teams, be the
head of a project, initiate activities, and be free to lead a team in
the way they think best.

Cholerics excel at confrontation. In fact, they're kind of like
pit bulls. They have no problem confronting issues .They state
what they feel openly and unashamedly. In fact, they feel that's the
best way to converse with someone—be straight about the issue.
To them, speaking to others in an open and candid way is simply
their way of being productive and honest. To others, it might come
off cocky, arrogant, rude, personal, and offensive. But they don't
see it that way! They actually believe being candid is being honest
and is the best form of communication. So, before being offended
by them, understand how their brain is wired.

If you think you or someone on your team might be a choleric,
take a look at a few of the following strengths and weaknesses. In
fact, you'll want to take an inventory of every member on your
team. You have my permission to copy the chart of the strengths
and weaknesses you see in this chapter that typically characterizes
the Choleric, the Sanguine, The Melancholy, and the Phlegmatic.
Make a list of each team member, then take a look at the following
characteristics of each personality. If someone seems to have a
majority of these characteristics, they're more than likely that type
of personality.

Place a check mark next to the quality that characterizes
them most.

THE _STRENGTHS_ OF A CHOLERIC:

☐ Born Leader	☐ Lacks Mercy	☐ Resourceful	☐ Black and White
☐ Confident	☐ Persuasive	☐ Self-Reliant	☐ Daring
☐ Strong-Willed	☐ Positive	☐ Corrects Wrong	☐ Loves Competition
☐ Competitive	☐ Embraces Change	☐ Independent	☐ Must Prove Wrong
☐ Speaks Openly	☐Forceful	☐ Quick Decisions	☐ Needs Few Friends
☐ Discourage-Proof	☐ Productive	☐ Takes Risks	☐ Charges Ahead

THE _WEAKNESSES_ OF A CHOLERIC:

☐ Bossy	☐ Unsympathetic	☐ Resistant
☐ Frank	☐ Impatient	☐ Unaffectionate
☐ Egotistical	☐ Proud	☐ Argumentative
☐ Frustrated with Others	☐ Workaholic	☐ Tactless
☐ Domineering	☐ Intolerant	☐ Manipulative
☐ Stubborn	☐ Lord over Others	☐ Short-tempered

Take this inventory and see if you can identify the Cholerics on your team!

A WORD ABOUT CHOLERICS

A Choleric thinks in terms of "black and white." There are very few gray areas. They call it like they see it. They don't hold back. To them, it's a waste of time and energy to go down any other path. In the process of doing so, however, to the others on the team who don't possess this personality trait they appear to throw diplomacy and mercy out the window.

If you're a Choleric, you have to remember that there are other personality types who don't think like you do. They are sensitive to what's being said to them. Just because you've been wired a different way, you must take into account that your team members ARE wired differently. You must respect that in the same way you expect them to respect your personality style. They value the feelings and words coming from other people to such a degree they feel words should be used in a diplomatic and respectful fashion. If you start blurting out exactly how you feel without considering how others might perceive it, you're definitely going to offend someone. You might say, "Who cares? They need to get over it." But that type of attitude only makes things worse. As a leader of a peak performance team, your job is to pull people together, working as a unit synergistically. If you take the attitude that says, "If it works for me, then it ought to work for everybody else," then you're headed for a mutiny.

If you're not a Choleric, you can still be a peak performance leader, too. If Cholerics had the role of supervisor in every business around the world, it would be a dangerous thing! It takes all types of personalities to make an organization run efficiently and effectively.

WORKING WITH A CHOLERIC

One thing I've heard and often seen while speaking to managers and supervisors across the country, is that quite often having a Choleric on the team can appear to be a threat to the leader, especially if they're not a Choleric themselves. Since Cholerics are of an aggressive nature and usually appear egotistical about things (i.e.; a know-it-all), they can intimidate the leader. Often, people within the team gravitate to someone with a strong personality, making the leader feel that the Choleric is dividing the group and manufacturing a hostile takeover.

As a leader, the best thing you could do is to discuss this feeling openly and honestly with the Choleric. Keep in mind, the Choleric relates to an open and honest conversation. So you need to do the same. You need to speak their language! They appreciate the more assertive approach to communications, because that's how they think it should be done. They hate to waste time on small talk. This is NOT an encouragement to be rude or to speak without tact and respect. You must speak respectfully to the Choleric, even if they aren't able to.

If you find yourself in a disagreement with a Choleric, you're in for a fight. They usually think in terms of win-lose, where they win and you lose. Since they often lack diplomacy skills, they find it difficult and at times irrational to think a disagreement could actually end up in a win-win situation.

As you approach your disagreement with a Choleric, I'd like to provide you a word of caution. Be assertive, but not argumentative. You'll only make matters worse. Back up your disagreement with facts and documentation. Because of their "know-it-all" attitude, they'll respond more affirmatively if you can prove you are correct. They'll have more respect for your disagreement if backed up with sound documentation and proof.

If you have a Choleric on your team, the most ideal environment for them would be the following:

- Freedom from controls, supervision, and details.

- An innovative and futuristic-oriented environment.

- A forum in which they can readily express their ideas and viewpoints.

- An environment devoid of routine work. They love to innovate.

- They enjoy new challenges and new opportunities.

One of my dearest friends was ecstatic when he married a Choleric/Melancholy. That means that she predominantly carries with her the personality of a Choleric and at times and in certain circumstances characterizes the personality of a Melancholy. Circumstances and events dictate which dominant personality plays forth. You're probably the same way!

My friend is a pure Sanguine. As you can see, they are opposites. Most couples are. When they first started dating, he couldn't believe how much they were alike. After they got married, I had to laugh when he said to me, "I married my opposite!"

That's how it is. Married couples seem to work that way. We are subconsciously attracted to those who support our weaknesses. Opposites do attract!

As a married couple, they had to adjust to each other's personality. By learning each other's personality style, they began to understand the "why" about each other. She understood why he didn't see the need to check his online banking statement (which was unbelievable to her), on a regular basis, and he understood why she was always trying to make the house look as perfect as she could. She understood that God didn't hard-wire him to be naturally prone to thinking in terms of details. He eventually learned why she demanded the house be "perfect" all the time. She was more rigid about control, while he was more relaxed. They both understand the "why." They didn't always like it or agree with it, but understanding how they were made gave them room to allow for what each of them saw as shortcomings. He wasn't yelling at her to relax more and she wasn't nagging him about all the details. They understood each other and respected each other's God-given shape and talent.

Having that kind of knowledge about each other's personality will help you go farther in your marriage, and in your relationship with others on the team. It will help you discover the "why" of an individual.

Since we're talking about Cholerics, let me end with a few more things about them. The Choleric has some definite developmental issues when it comes to working with a team. The first important thing they need to keep in mind is that they need the team. They may think they're carrying the team, but the truth is the team is carrying them.

Another developmental flaw is that the Choleric is usually only interested in their personal needs and goals. The team can often get in the way of their personal drive. These types of Cholerics will often work against the interests of the team, believing that their ideas and strategies are best for the team.

Under stress, the Choleric can become impulsive, hot-tempered, demanding, and dictatorial. Some Cholerics may even choose to live in the extreme elements of their style, becoming the classic "difficult person." When that happens, yelling, bullying, demanding, and even physically aggressive actions can result. As a leader, this must be addressed as quickly as possible!

Cholerics can also be praise-challenged. They're not prone to praising people well. They do notice when people do a good job, but it is not a natural inclination to praise it. The Choleric sees good or even great work as something everyone should be doing and is a natural part of the job requirement. When seen from this perspective, they don't see the need for praise. It was expected of the person to do a great job.

To be a peak performance Choleric, you need to work at recognizing the strengths of others, listen to your team, consider their advice as something valuable, care about them and let them know you care with praise and rewards, be careful with your words, work hard at being merciful and patient, and stop being a know it all.

THE HAPPY SANGUINE

Of all the personality styles, the Sanguine is the easiest to be around socially. Sanguines are extroverts. They are the outgoing, optimistic, cheerful person that brings energy to a room or to a team. They are always trying to find the positive in all things. The glass is always half full. They love to dream, set goals, and live life to the fullest. While they excel at being outgoing, warm, compassionate, and can make friends easily, they have a tough time with maintaining friendships because of their inability to stay on task and commitments.

Let's take a better look at how the Sanguines are hard-wired:

THE _STRENGTHS_ OF A SANGUINE:

☐ Optimistic	☐ Charismatic	☐ Touchy	☐ Colorful
☐ Social	☐ Friendly	☐ High Energy	☐ Star of the Show
☐ Loves People	☐ Loves Attention	☐ Inspirational	☐ A Good Starter
☐ Cheerleader	☐ Likes Change	☐ Sense of Humor	☐ Apologetic
☐ Motivator	☐ Sensitive	☐ Helpful	☐ Volunteering
☐ Emotional	☐ Conflict Resolver	☐ Team Player	☐ Adventuresome

THE _WEAKNESSES_ OF A SANGUINE:

☐ Talkative	☐ Restless Energy	☐ Wastes Time
☐ Too happy for some	☐ Controlled by Circumstances	☐ No Follow Through
☐ Easily hurt	☐ Superficial in Relationships	☐ Appears Flashy
☐ Egotistical	☐ Rather talk than work	☐ Wants the Credit
☐ Exaggerates	☐ Confidence Fades Fast	☐ Dominates Talk	
☐ Can't remember names	☐ Easily Distracted	☐ Repeat Stories

Take the inventory and see if you can identify the Sanguines on your team!

A WORD ABOUT SANGUINES

The Sanguine is the happiest of all personalities, and the best at bringing people together for a common cause. They are the next in line for those who might seem to be a natural born leader. Because of their charisma, many people think they are natural born leaders.

They are the most people-oriented type of person on the planet. They exude enthusiasm. They may not have more talent or opportunity than any other personality type but they usually end up having more fun. They love people, parties, and attention. They're comfortable on a stage and relating stories, events, or any kind of chatter to others. They are the most natural conflict-resolution mediator known to man due to their natural people skills. They can deflate hostilities and help negotiate a common ground. They get their "high" by motivating, inspiring, teaching, training, and working with people – the larger the group the better.

If a team succeeds, the Sanguine will give credit to the team. "I got where I am today because I build good relationships and make sure that people are taken care of." These Sanguines measure their work and their lives in terms of the quality of their relationships with others.

You'll find that many of them will gravitate into sales, a speaking career, politics, or any front end task that allows them to converse with people and share their ideas and feelings.

There are no strangers to Sanguines. While others hesitate or hold back, the Sanguine is usually the first to start up a conversation, say hello or to make friends with the person at the checkout counter.

I am a Sanguine and my kids used to hate it. They are often dreaded my presence at the local grocery store. I would stand around and talk to everyone—forever.

Many years ago, while on vacation at a resort, my children and I approached an elevator, which had several people on it. Immediately, my kids began begging me not to talk to anyone on the elevator. They just wanted to get on, go down to the first floor, and get off. But not me! Immediately, upon entering into the elevator I initiated the first "Good morning. How's everybody doing?" You could see the frustrated look in my kids' face. "There he goes again!" they were thinking, "Won't he ever stop talking to people?"

But those same kids of mine loved my personality when we were in a new setting and they were feeling a little bashful about meeting new people. They could always count on me to break the ice and get the conversation flowing.

Today, they love the fact that I can calm them down in a crisis, offer good solutions to their problems, feel compassionate about their needs, be playful while on vacation, find adventure everywhere we go, and be encouraging about the their future dreams and goals.

WORKING WITH SANGUINES

When it comes to the workplace, the Sanguine does well, ranging from staff positions to leadership. While the Sanguine doesn't have the driving passion for leadership like the Choleric, they still make excellent leaders because of their people skills, especially when balanced with personal assertiveness. Their leadership style is democratic, and when it comes to decision making, they are more concerned with making the right decision than with a quick one.

They have a strong need to be liked and praised. Making sure that the team comes to a consensus is important to a Sanguine. They are very uncomfortable with disagreements and conflict. As a leader, they struggle with being disliked and having to deal with problematic people. They want to please everybody. Receiving negative feelings from others is a real challenge, because they thrive on people liking them. Since people are at the center of their world, they need to know that people are happy with them. That's why they thrive on compliments from the boss and from the team. Rewards, praise, special recognition are all important to a Sanguine. When they do encounter difficult people or hurtful conversations, they're good about not holding grudges and can easily forgive. However, they often let pain and hurt feelings stay with them for a long time. They don't do well with hurt feelings. A crushed spirit can sideline them from moving forward that can affect their job performance and their personal lives.

The ideal environment for the Sanguine is to have a high degree of people contacts. They want freedom from control, freedom from movement, and a platform in which to share their ideas.

The challenges of the Sanguine are plenty, just like every other personality style.

They are great at getting things started, but they can easily get side-tracked and lack follow-through on a project. To them, starting a project is fun, but finishing can be a difficult chore. They are easily distracted and bored with things.

Another thing that comes as a challenge to a Sanguine is they like to talk too much. At the office, Sanguines often feel the need to spend five minutes of conversation with someone for every twenty minutes of focused mental activity. Since they are people-oriented, they need to interact with people more often than any other personality.

Sanguines especially like meetings because it brings people together and provides for a forum for them to discuss their ideas with other people. Unfortunately, due to their talkative nature, they can easily get off the point of the subject matter and chat their way down a rabbit trail.

Another challenge for the Sanguine is their memory. They can remember faces, numbers, and facts extremely well, but the ability to remember names and dates is very difficult. I know this must sound very strange, but my wife was constantly amazed at how my memory works. She used to be dumbfounded by how well I remembered people's phone numbers, their faces, and how well I could remember trivia about countries, people, science, politics, etc. But, what she couldn't understand was how I could remember a few things on a grocery list. She's amazed that out of the five things she sent me to the grocery store for, I could only remember three of them.

As far as names are concerned, I've learned to master it. However, earlier in my life, I struggled with remembering people's names. Today, I can meet 50 people coming into a room and remember all of their names. It has taken a lot of practice, and people are often amazed at my interest and ability to remember who they are. If only they knew the real me. I've worked hard to fix my challenges, and this is what you must do too!

When it comes to stressful moments during work, the tendency for a Sanguine is to be overly optimistic and unrealistic. This is when they really need to the help of a Melancholy to provide a balanced view. Under stress, the Sanguine can also be self-promoting and talkative.

Whatever you do as a leader, do not put a Sanguine over detailed work. They aren't generally good with details. They frustrate Melancholies with their non-detailed information during meetings, lack of preparation, overly unrealistic ideals and goals, and can't stand much of their small talk.

While a Sanguine is a popular person, and usually the kind of people voted as 'The Most Likely To Succeed,' they seldom succeed in the way you thought they would have. Success is not elusive to a Sanguine, it's just that with all their charm and people talent, most people expect them to go farther than they do. They have the ideas, the personality, the creativity, but many seldom get it all pulled together at any given time. If they happen to hit instant success, they ride high, but if it takes years of planning and hard work, they will quit and head off in another direction. Many Sanguines change jobs, even careers, every few years because they see the crown is elusive in this kingdom, so they'd better move on.

THE PERFECT MELANCHOLY

Now, let's take a look at the Perfect Melancholy personality. The Melancholy person is more of an introvert style. They are deep, thoughtful, and analytical people who love to have fun, are genuinely kind to others, and can appreciate the beauty of art, architecture, and the details of life.

Melancholies make great leaders when details are a critical component to success. They are great at structuring their time, their notes, and take great pride in keeping things organized and tidy.

There are more geniuses born with the Melancholy personality style than there is with other personality style. They love to think introspectively. Charts, graphs, figures, and lists excite them. They also love to finish what they start.

Melancholies gravitate to everything that requires efficiency and details. They lead architectural firms, accounting firms, and software firms. They make great doctors, attorneys, and technicians. They are inventors, musicians, and problem-solvers. They are happiest when high standards of efficiency are met, however many of them are such perfectionists that satisfaction can be out of reach for them.

Let's take a better look at what makes up the personality of a Melancholy:

THE *STRENGTHS* OF A MELANCHOLY:

☐ Analytical	☐ Considerate	☐ Chart-Maker	☐ Inventor
☐ Detail-Oriented	☐ Methodical	☐ Reserved	☐ Needs Facts
☐ Perfectionist	☐ Sensitive	☐ Thinker	☐ Needs Proof
☐ Orderly	☐ Planner	☐ Introspective	☐ Deep Thought
☐ Persistent	☐ Scheduled	☐ Technical	☐ Fixer Upper
☐ Self-Sacrificing	☐ Musical	☐ Team Player	☐ Quiet

THE *WEAKNESSES* OF A MELANCHOLY:

☐ High Standards	☐ Critical	☐ Suspicious
☐ Perfectionist	☐ Hard To Please	☐ Loner
☐ Fussy	☐ Insecure	☐ Indecisive
☐ Pessimistic	☐ Withdrawn	☐ Careful Thinker
☐ Negative Attitude	☐ Depressed	☐ Bashful
☐ Unforgiving	☐ Moody	☐ Argumentative

Take the inventory and see if you can identify the Melancholies on your team!

A WORD ABOUT MELANCHOLIES

There's a wide range of Melancholy behavior, but all Melancholies have a focus on details and processes. Their ability to stay organized is very critical to their work and success. They rely on things being under control. They emphasize the importance of having a detailed plan and that everything they do is thorough. They are great at developing processes that need to be systematic, well documented, and in compliance with policy. As long as the process is correctly followed, they feel comfortable that the desired results will be obtained. They love charts, graphs, and any extra information that might seem superfluous to other personality styles.

Melancholies are usually found in management roles when details and process management are critical ingredients for success. They tend to hold staff positions including accounting, quality assurance, and technical support, where these kinds of strengths are essential.

Aristotle once said, "All men of Genius are of Melancholy temperament." Melancholy personalities are deep thinkers. They are more serious about life. They see themselves as realists, and are typically the most talented and creative of all the temperaments. Most of your writers, artists, and musicians are of a Melancholy personality.

Michelangelo was undoubtedly a Melancholy. Before he carved his classic statues of Moses, David, and The Pieta, he made an intensive study of the human body. He went to the morgues and cut up the cadavers to study the muscles and sinews. Because he went deeper into the details of design than the average sculptor of his day, his creations are protected and respected to this day.

Melancholies enjoy the details of life. They feel that they are critical to life itself. They are thrilled with things that are artistic, musical, philosophical, poetic, and literary in nature. They appreciate gifted people, admire geniuses, and admit an occasional tear of emotion. They are moved by the greats of all mediums, and they marvel at the wonder of nature.

Melancholies also think that lists, charts, and graphs are an essential part of life.

WORKING WITH A MELANCHOLY

Melancholies have an indirect and task-oriented style. They are slower-paced, which is part of their methodical approach. They like to take time to think it through before they take action.

This can often frustrate others who aren't as detail-oriented. Melancholies are frustrated when others don't seem to understand the need for thorough thought. They are also frustrated when people don't seem to respect the rules, agree with policy, follow procedures, and coordinate themselves with systems that are set up to manage the work.

A cartoon by Colman titled "Men and Women" shows a couple facing each other. He looks depressed and she says, "If this is happy, what are you like when you're sad?" With the Melancholy person, it is sometimes hard to tell happy from sad, because they don't want to get too excited, and most of life is serious - if not downright depressing.

The Melancholy is so serious about life that they tend to take everything too personally. If they hear their names across the room, they're convinced people are talking about them. They are frustrated by the loud, powerful Choleric who wants to get things done fast and at backbreaking paces. They don't really care for the Sanguines, either. They see them too unrealistic about life and are somewhat naive. Although they appreciate their positive attitude and fun-loving style, they abhor their lack of attention to detail and processes.

While speaking at a marriage conference several years ago, a wife shared with me how she was having a very difficult time understanding her husband. She mentioned she was raised by a father who was a detail-oriented perfectionist. She grew up in a home where everything was in perfect order. Having inherited her father's perfectionist style, she easily understood the need for having things in order. Each day, she watched her father fix his own cars, fix any and all gadgets around the house, do things more efficiently than anyone else, and do all he could do to get things done without spending a penny for it. He prided himself in that. That was her understanding of a man and how things should be.

Shortly after she got married, she realized her husband was the opposite of her perfectionist style. If things needed fixing around the house, he told her he would call the "fix-it" guy. If the oil needed changing, he found it easier to take it to the shop rather than do it himself. Again, "Time is money," he thought. To him, spending money on the expert who enjoys doing those kinds of things and has the ability to do it, was a smart choice.

After hearing me speak on personalities at the marriage conference, they felt a huge sigh of relief. She thought something was wrong with him. He thought she demanded way too much from him. Once they learned how they were designed by their Creator to have personalities that complimented each other, they were committed to understanding each other better and being more gracious with each other's weaknesses.

The Melancholy have many challenges. One challenge is their negative attitude. They can be very pessimistic about life. Their mind is like a radio dial that's set on negative. What they need to do is to practice looking at the positive things in life. People hate to be around a grouch.

Melancholies need to work on procrastination. It's a challenge for them. Because of their perfectionist tendencies, they often refrain from starting certain projects because they are afraid they won't do them right. While the Phlegmatic procrastinates in hopes they won't have to do it, the Melancholy holds back because they have to do it perfectly.

Melancholies also tend to spend too much time in the planning stage. In my management training conferences, one of the frustrations that was consistently discussed about Melancholies was how aggravated team members were when the Melancholy took too much time to plan. They often want to plan it out so thoroughly that the project inevitably got delayed. When this happened, customers and team members ended up very unhappy. The team members suffered, because it held them up on getting the product to the customer as promised. The customers got angry, because the integrity of the deadline had been tainted.

Melancholies need to relax their standards a bit. While everyone appreciates their talent in doing things right, their standard of excellence can often be set much too high and be unrealistic to meet.

Several years ago, I met a wonderful, gracious young man who was an optometrist and a Melancholy. He was very gifted in his practice and was dating a beautiful, young lady from our church. He was deeply in love with her and had made several attempts over the course of a year to marry her, but would always back out of their engagement shortly after he would make the decision to get married.

One day, he came to me for counsel and asked me what I thought he should do. I asked him, "What is it about her that makes you want to marry her and then suddenly back out a day or two later?" I couldn't believe what he said to me. At first, he went on and on about how wonderful she was and how beautiful he thought she looked. I agreed. Then, he made this statement, "Yes, she's all those things, but she's not perfect!" Wow! I couldn't believe what I was hearing. Here was a guy who thought this woman was practically a goddess, but because she wasn't exactly perfect, he couldn't bring himself to marry her.

I asked him, "Are you someone who considers yourself a realist?" He responded and answered, "Yes, as a matter of fact, I am."

"If you're a realist, then how come you're being so unrealistic?" I shot back. "Do you actually believe there are perfect people here on this planet? Do you actually think you'll find a perfect woman? And, besides that, do you feel justified in requiring a perfect mate simply because you're so perfect?"

He chuckled at my question and sheepishly said, "No, I realize there's no one who's perfect, and I'm not perfect. I just want to make sure she's the right one."

"Believe me," I said, "If she's put up with your off-and-on again engagement tactics and she still wants to marry you, she's the right one. In my opinion, she's as perfect as they come!"

Sadly, he never married her. His standards were too high.

THE PATIENT PHLEGMATIC

The fourth personality type is the patient Phlegmatic. The Phlegmatic, like the Melancholy, is an introvert. They naturally maintain a low-key personality that's easy going, calm, cool, relaxed, and usually very quiet. They are reserved people who like to stay in the background and watch. They almost never say anything in a meeting. They would rather listen than to be heard.

Although they are quiet people, when they do speak it usually carries weight and can be witty. They make great leaders when the environment is extremely hectic. They have the natural ability to remain calm under pressure. They're never in a hurry and they seldom get upset. This is the kind of person who makes a great parent. They are very patient with kids and will be patient with the team.

At work, they are great with administrative duties and/or mediation issues. No one is as good a listener as the Phlegmatic. They love to listen to others. Sitting at the mall watching people all day is fun to them. Listening to you describe all the details of your 4-week vacation is pure joy. Since they are so peaceful and agreeable, they also get along with just about everybody. Everybody is their friend. Without a doubt, they are your all-purpose person and one of the best team players you'll ever find.

Let's take a closer look at the Phlegmatic:

THE _STRENGTHS_ OF A PHLEGMATIC:

☐ Peaceful	☐ Friendly	☐ Content
☐ Easy Going	☐ Diplomatic	☐ Pleasant
☐ Controlled	☐ Consistent	☐ Satisfied
☐ Submissive	☐ Great Listener	☐ Balanced
☐ Patient	☐ Dry Humor	☐ Quiet
☐ Shy	☐ Mediator	

THE _WEAKNESSES_ OF A PHLEGMATIC:

☐ Blank	☐ Nonchalant	☐ Mumbles
☐ Unenthusiastic	☐ Worrier	☐ Loner
☐ Indecisive	☐ Lazy	☐ Doubtful
☐ Uninvolved	☐ Slow	☐ Reluctant
☐ Hesitant	☐ Withdrawn	☐ Bashful
☐ Plain	☐ Sluggish	☐ Avoids Conflict

Take the inventory and see if you can identify the Phlegmatic on your team!

A WORD ABOUT PHLEGMATIC

The Phlegmatic is the easiest of all temperaments to get along with. They are probably the closest thing there is to a balanced person. They don't typically function in the extremes or excesses of life, but walk solidly down the middle road. They like to avoid conflict and ensure a balanced environment. The Phlegmatic person does not offend or call attention to him or herself, but will quietly do what is expected of him without looking for credit. While the Choleric is the "born leader", the Phlegmatic is the "learned leader," and with proper motivation, they can rise to the top due to their outstanding ability to get along with everybody else.

These peaceful Phlegmatics are always calm and slow to anger. They seem to be in control of stress at all times and are never impulsive. This is perhaps their most admirable quality, to stay calm under pressure. If you had an incident where the Sanguines would scream, the Cholerics would lash out, and the Melancholies would sink into depression, the Phlegmatic rides a cool wave. He backs up and waits a minute, and then moves quietly in the right direction. Emotion does not overwhelm the Phlegmatic, and anger doesn't enter his or her heart.

Because the Choleric is noted as the typical business executive, we sometimes overlook the Phlegmatic as a competent, steady worker—one who gets along with everyone and has administrative ability.

During a tumultuous time in our nation, immediately following the Watergate scandal of President Nixon, the United States selected a peaceful man, a Phlegmatic to take his place and calm a disturbed nation. That man was Gerald Ford.

Bob Pierpoint of CBS once said about Gerald Ford, "Jerry Ford is decent, friendly, and compassionate. He didn 't really have a new or progressive thought in twenty-five years, but he's a genuinely good guy." Author Doris Goodwin called him "enjoyable, unassuming, relaxed, easygoing, well balanced, normal, decent, honest, regular." The All-American Mr. Clean.

It was Ford's middle-of-the-road, totally inoffensive nature that caused him to be chosen at a moment in history when we didn't want a flashy, daring question mark, but a simple, solid man we could trust.

In any area of life, there is some conflict: parent/child; teacher/pupil; boss/employee; friend/friend. As the other temperaments strain and strike, the Phlegmatic tries to keep peace in the ranks. As men struggle on choppy waters, the Phlegmatic lifts his head and calms the seas. As others fight for their own way, the Phlegmatic sits back and gives objective opinions. Every home and business needs at least one Phlegmatic to look at both sides and provide a calm, cool, and collected reply.

WORKING WITH A PHLEGMATIC

The Phlegmatic makes an incredible friend because his total assets add up to positive human relations. Due to his easygoing, relaxed, calm, cool, well/balanced, patient, consistent, peaceful, inoffensive, and pleasant temperament, everyone is attracted to him. Quite frankly, the Phlegmatic seldom has an enemy. The Phlegmatic will work hard to be a friend to everyone. If they know of someone who's been offended by something they have done, they will make it a priority to make it right with that individual. What more could anyone ask for in a friend?

As with each type of temperament, the types of strengths have corresponding weaknesses. Because the Phlegmatic has low-key strengths, they also have low-key weaknesses.

Since the Phlegmatic is a very relaxed individual, they are often seen as lacking motivation. They are often seen as lazy; and the extreme form of a Phlegmatic is a tendency to be lazy and to procrastinate about work.

The problem of procrastination is prevalent with both the Melancholy and the Phlegmatic, but for different reasons. The Melancholy doesn't want to do the work until he or she has all of the right information in order to do the job correctly. The Phlegmatic, on the other hand, postpones the job simply because he or she doesn't want to do it at all.

Having this relaxed frame of mind, they also tend to have a difficult time establishing priorities and making a decision about things. They are prone to being the most democratic of all personalities. They want to hear all sides communicate before making a decision. Due to their grit-iron determination to please everyone, they tend to stall for a decision. They don't want to hurt anyone's feelings and they'll do anything possible to avoid controversy.

Another danger of the Phlegmatic temperament is their willingness to do it all to please the leader. They will take on more than they can handle. They make a great team player. They are willing to do whatever needs to be done for the leader and the cause. However, in the process, they will also overload themselves with too many tasks. For a person who tends to procrastinate and has a difficult time making decisions, as a leader you'll want to make sure the Phlegmatic doesn't overload themselves.

Here's another way to view the four different personalities as they relate to the people who work on your team.

A COLLECTIVE LOOK
AT THE FOUR TEMPERAMENTS

	CHOLERIC	SANGUINE	MELANCHOLY	PHLEGMATIC
Likes to: *Wants to know:*	Focus (What) Task at hand	Relates (Who) The big picture	Integrates (Why) Its significance	Operates (How) The details
Preferred roles:	Take charge	Coordinate	Problem solving	Monitoring
Concerned with:	Practicality	Teamwork	Innovation	Documentation
Manages by:	Directing	Organizing	Planning	Controlling
Leader style:	Authoritative	Democratic	Self-directed	Systematic
Wants to be:	Productive	Flexible	Self-reliant	Accountable
Values: *Follows:*	Experience Strong leader	Participation The group	Questioning Personal reason	Compliance Policy
Works well:	WI clear goals	WI broad goals	WI ideas/input	WI systems
Focus is on:	Outcomes	Involvement	Input	Procedures
Wants to have:	Authority	Influence	Time to assess	Boundaries
Learns by:	Doing	Observing	Listening	Repetition

Chapter 8
You Can Do It

Motivational speaker Earl Nightingale used to tell a story about a little boy named Sparky, who failed at nearly everything he tried. School was impossible for Sparky. In the eighth grade, he failed every single subject. In high school, he fared no better-flunking physics, Latin, algebra, and English. Sparky was no jock, either. In fact, he was horrible at sports. He finally managed to make the golf team, but lost the only important match that he competed in. There was a "consolation" match, but he lost that, too.

Sparky also had trouble on the social front. He just didn't have any social skills. He was awkward around other people, and generally ignored by his classmates. He went through his entire high school years without ever dating anyone. Everyone agreed that if you looked up the word "loser" in the dictionary, it would probably show a picture of Sparky.

The only one thing that Sparky enjoyed doing was draw. He liked his artwork. The problem was nobody else did. He submitted cartoons to the school yearbook, and was promptly rejected. But despite these setbacks, Sparky decided to become a professional artist. After high school, he sent some of his cartoons to Walt Disney Studios. He was rejected again.

Rather than give up, though, Sparky pressed on. This time, he decided to write his own autobiography in cartoons. He told the story of a little round-faced boy who failed at everything he tried. He couldn't fly a kite, he couldn't kick a football...and he couldn't do anything right.

Of course, that little boy in the comic strip was Charlie Brown. And Sparky was none other than Charles Schultz, who created the "Peanuts" strip, arguably the most successful comic strip of all time.

There's something to be said for tenacity. If you'll keep working hard at developing a peak performance team, you'll eventually end up there, but it won't come without hardships.

I like what former President Richard Nixon said when commenting on the subject of success, "Success is not a harbor but a voyage with its own perils to the spirit. The game of life is to come up a winner, to be a success, or to achieve what we set out to do. Yet there is always the danger of failure as a human being. The lesson that most of us on this voyage never learn, but can never forget, is that to win is sometimes to lose."

There will be difficult moments on your journey to developing a peak performance team, but stick it out anyway. Don't quit. You can think about it, but don't quit. Whatever strides you make, no matter how long it takes to reach your destination of peak performance, you will be better off than where you originally were.

As Earl Nightingale puts it, "Success is the progressive realization of a worthy goal or ideal." As long as you are progressing, that's the main thing.

"Your task, to build a better world," God said.

I answered, "How? The world is such a large vast place and so complicated now. And I so small and useless am. There's nothing I can do."

But God in all His wisdom said, "Just build a better you."

Personal Profile

Randy Shepard is a nationally-known management consultant, trainer, and speaker. His clients have included such corporate giants as Wal-Mart, AT&T, Sprint, Delta Dental, and The U.S. Department of Agriculture. Randy regularly conducts personal and corporate growth seminars to equip people with the practical tools on such subjects as leadership, teamwork, conflict resolution, and employee motivation.

Throughout his years as a trainer and lecturer, Randy has also had the privilege of ministering to nearly 600 churches throughout the country. In 1994, Randy came off the road to start a new church in the Kansas City area where he was pastor for five years. Today, it continues to be one of the fastest growing churches in the state.

Randy is the father of three adult children and five grandchildren. He resides in the Kansas City metro area.